HAMLET

William Shakespeare

PEACOCK BOOKS

Published by
PEACOCK BOOKS
7/22, Ansari Road, Darya Ganj, New Delhi-110002
Phones : +91-11-40775252, 40775214, 23273880, 23275880
Fax : +91-11-23285873
Web : www.atlanticbooks.com
E-mail : orders@atlanticbooks.com

Peacock Books is an imprint of
Atlantic Publishers and Distributors (P) Ltd

First published 1603

Printed & bound in India by Atlantic Print Services

CONTENTS

SHAKESPEARE'S PLAYS WITH THEIR PROBABLE APPROXIMATE DATES

There is absence of total agreement on the dates of Shakespearean plays. Some scholars give an earlier date than the one suggested here for Shakespeare's first play. Doubt also remains concerning the actual order of composition in particular years. Having stated that, the editor gives hereunder the approximate dates as largely accepted by Shakespeare scholars in general.

1590-91

Henry VI Part II
Henry VI Part III

1591-92

Henry VI Part I

1592-93

Richard III
Comedy of Errors

1593-94

Titus Andronicus
Taming of the Shrew

1594-95

Two Gentlemen of Verona
Love's Labour's Lost
Romeo and Juliet

1595-96

Richard II
Midsummer Night's Dream

1596-97

King John
Merchant of Venice

1597-98

Henry IV Part I
Henry IV Part II

1598-99

Much Ado About Nothing
Henry V

1599-1600

Julius Caesar
As You Like It
Twelfth Night

1600-1601

Hamlet

Merry Wives of Windsor

1601-02

Troilus and Cressida

1602-03

All's Well That Ends Well

1604-05

Measure for Measure

Othello

1605-06

King Lear

Macbeth

1606-07

Antony and Cleopatra

1607-08

Coriolanus

Timon of Athens

1608-09

Pericles

1609-10

Cymbeline

1610-11

Winter's Tale

1611-12

The Tempest

1612-13

Henry VIII

Two Noble Kinsmen

WILLIAM SHAKESPEARE

Biographical Sketch

1. A Symbol of Culture

Introducing Shakespeare to the general reader, G.B. Harrison begins his book with the following statement:

> No household in the English-speaking world is properly furnished unless it contains copies of the *Holy Bible* and of *The Works of William Shakespeare*. It is not always thought necessary that these books should be read in maturer years, but they must be present as symbols of Religion and Culture.

Not only in the English speaking world, but everywhere, acquaintance with Shakespeare's plays is regarded as a mark of culture; and there is hardly any language-community in the civilized world, which does not possess Shakespeare in translation.

2. Life

Anyone looking for reliable historical information about Shakespeare is bound to meet with disappointment. We get very little help from his contemporaries in the form of recorded reference allusion, or memoirs, Shakespeare himself is completely silent about himself, and as regards his works, he has consumed himself into them so perfectly that it is very risky to draw any clear inferences from his works—except, perhaps, the sonnets, some of which, departing from the convention, appear to be expressing personal experience. We do, however, get some definite information from the parish register, legal documents and town records.

At first sight, it may appear astonishing that such a great writer as Shakespeare should have received no notice from his contemporaries and that no attempt should have been made to preserve every bit of the records associated with his life. But a second look at the state of affairs and attitude to biography prevailing in that period will mollify our uneasiness. The Elizabethans, generally, were indifferent to biographical and autobiographical notes and memoirs; even the biography of the most important personage, Queen Elizabeth herself, is full of gaps and guesses. It should, in fact, be gratifying that we possess more of authentic information about Shakespeare than about any of his contemporary writers excepting Ben Jonson. Moreover, Shakespeare, until very late in his life, was a very ordinary individual belonging to the socially unwelcome profession of actor; and the playwrights, too, were not much distinguished in the society. The critical response to his work was not unmixed high praise until the end of the eighteenth century. It was only in the beginning of the nineteenth century that Shakespeare became established as a great writer who must be spoken of with a feeling of reverence. But during the intervening centuries, he had been steadily moving towards the highest position, and as this process advanced, his admirers became over enthusiastic to complete his biography. The result was an infusion of a great deal of guesswork aggrandisement and romanticising. In such a situation, the best policy will be to keep close to the attested facts and reasonable inferences, except in cases where a highly dubious anecdote may, nevertheless, indicate some important turn in the dramatist's life.

William Shakespeare—the surname is found spelled in various other ways, which was not unusual in those days—was the son of John Shakespeare of Stratford-on-Avon. In 1556

John Shakespeare bought a house in Henley Street. In 1552, he, along with two neighbours, had been fined for keeping an unauthorized dunghill on Henley Street, which means he had been dwelling there for some years before he bought the house. In 1557 he married Mary Arden, the daughter of Robert Arden, a land-owning farmer who lived in Wilmcote, a small village two miles from Stratford. Mary brought with her an inheritance of sixty acres of land.

John Shakespeare was a glove-maker and dealer in wool, he may have at one time or another, pursued some other trades as well. He was a prosperous citizen of Stratford and one of its notables.

In the year of William Shakespeare's birth, however, his father was a prosperous businessman who was also a man of substance and of social standing. William, the third and surviving child of John and Mary Shakespeare was baptized on 26 April 1564. Allowing the usual period of three days between birth and baptism, it is generally assumed that William Shakespeare was born on 23 April 1564, which is also the day of the feast of St. George, the patron saint of England—and this is also the day on which Shakespeare breathed his last. The Shakespeares had five more children. It requires no documentary evidence to say that Shakespeare during his childhood observed and absorbed the life of town and village surging all around him and, possessing a rare talent, he stored in his mind sights, sounds, scenes and characters, which, combined with his experience of London, would prove a rich material at the forge of his creativity, when he came to write poems and plays.

There is no valid reason to doubt that William was enrolled in the local grammar school when he was six or seven years old. His father was still a prominent citizen and an important member of the borough council. But the school records for the period are not available. Nicholas Rowe, who brought out the first edited collection of Shakespeare's plays, wrote in his introduction that the boy studied in a free school where "it is probable, he acquired what Latin he was master of, but the narrowness of his circumstances, and the want of his assistance at home, forced his father to withdraw him from thence, and unhappily prevented his further proficiency in that language". John Aubrey a seventeenth-century antiquarian and biographer, in his *Brief Lives* published posthumously in 1813, informs us that Shakespeare had been a school master in a country school.

There is, however, no confusion regarding his early marriage to Anne Hathaway, who was about eight years his senior. One thing that can be safely inferred is that Shakespeare was an impetuous and highly romantic young man and this conclusion gets ample support in the essential nature of all his writings—they are romantic through and through. On 26th May 1583, their first issue Susanna was baptized in Stratford and two years later, the twins, Hamnet and Judith were born and christened on 2 February 1585. Of these children of Shakespeare, Hamnet died in 1596, Susanna married a physician named John Hall and inherited a major portion of her father's assets, Judith married Thomas Quiney.

The period from 1585 to 1592 in Shakespeare's life is known as the "dark years" or "lost years" from the biographer's point of view. For this period we have no authentic information about the family apart from a single reference to John Shakespeare in 1588 in connection with a legal dispute over a sum of money. There is, however, no dearth of legend and hearsay. According to Nicholas Rowe, Shakespeare incurred the wrath of the local landlord, Sir Thomas Lucy for stealing deer in his park and was, as a result, obliged to flee to London.

Though there are many conjectures, yet what sounds most credible is that Shakespeare attached himself to one of the touring theatrical companies that visited the countryside during the period under consideration. Three such companies, the Earl of Worcester's Men, the Earl of Oxford's Men and the Earl of Essex's Men, were giving performances at Stratford in 1581 and in 1585 the town people were entertained by an unidentified company. In 1587, the year in which Shakespeare most probably left his home town, the Earl of Essex's Men and the Earl of Leicester's Men were in Stratford; he might have accompanied one of these groups to London.

In the midst of financial and other problems besetting the family, joining a company of actors must have appealed to Shakespeare as a good expedient because it would bring some wages as well as give him an access to the literary world of London.

By 1592 Shakespeare's struggle had begun to bear fruit; in that year he was worthy enough to arouse the jealousy of another playwright, Robert Greene, one of the University Wits. In a letter addressed to his fellow writers and appended to a pamphlet called *Greene's Groatsworth of Wit Bought with a Million of Repentance* he made a scurrilous attack on Shakespeare for presuming to be not only an actor but the best playwright.

It is clear that by 1592 Shakespeare had established himself in London as an actor and dramatist: he had completed at least the three plays comprising the *Henry VI* trilogy; he had also probably been improving and retouching existing plays and there might have been some talk of his writing then in progress. Some scholars have argued that he had also completed or was about to complete *The Two Gentlemen of Verona, The Comedy of Errors, The Taming of the Shrew, Richard III, Titus Andronicus* and *Love's Labour's Lost.*

The next year, 1593, saw the publication of a long narrative poem, *Venus and Adonis*, with a signed dedication to Henry Wriothesley, the third Earl of Southampton: Your Honour's in all duty, William Shakespeare." In the following year came out another poem, *The Rape of Lucrece*, also dedicated to the same lord. This was the period during which the London theatres remained closed on account of the plague; that Shakespeare did not waste his time, but was busy writing poetry shows with what earnestness he pursued his aim of achieving literary renown. He had also started writing his sonnets during this period and some scholars have suggested that the group of sonnets addressed to a young man had the Earl of Southampton for their inspirator.

The theatres reopened in 1594 and staging of plays including some by Shakespeare began. We find that he is already an important member of Lord Chamberlain's company as disclosed by the following entry in the Chamber Accounts:

> To William Kemp, William Shakespeare, and Richard Burbage, servants to the Lord Chamberlain, upon the Council's warrant dated at Whitehall 15 March 1594 (-5) for two several comedies or interludes showed by them before her Majesty in Christmas time last past, *viz.* upon St. Stephen's day and Innocent's day, £ 13 6s, 8d, and by way of her Majesty's reward £ 6 13s, 4d.

From recorded references, allusions and lists of actors prefixed to printed plays, we gather that Shakespeare continued to act on the stage at least up to 1603 and if we rely on his fellow-actors, John Heminge and Henry Condell, who edited the First Folio edition of his plays in 1623, up to 1611. He is said to have played kingly roles including the Ghost in *Hamlet* but he also acted the part of old servant Adam in *As You Like It*. According to Aubrey, he "did act exceedingly well".

All the while Shakespeare was making steady progress in writing plays and in earning money and fame. During 1595-96, five of his new plays were produced: *Richard II, Romeo and Juliet, King John, A Midsummer Night's Dream,* and *The Merchant of Venice*. During the latter year there was a tragedy in the family: his only son Hamnet died in August 1596. In the same year, there was some more trouble for Shakespeare: according to a reference discovered by Leslie Hotson in 1931, one William Wayt claimed sureties of the peace against William Shakespeare and some other persons including Francis Langley then owner of the Swan Theatre. But his financial position was quite sound. He was living in a large house in Bishopsgate as the tax-rolls indicate, perhaps his family also stayed with him for brief periods. There is evidence of his purchase of property in London and in his hometown.

While living in London, Shakespeare appears to have maintained good links with his native place and its people. His narrative poems had been printed by Richard Field who had migrated from Stratford. In 1597 Shakespeare bought the largest house in Stratford, called New Place, from William Underhill for a sum of £ 60. On October 25, 1598, Richard Quiney a Stratford man who was visiting London wrote a letter to Shakespeare requesting a loan of £ 30. In 1599 the famous actor, Richard Burbage and his brother Cuthbert set up a new playhouse on the Bankside, called the Globe. Since they could not finance the project on their own, they invited some other members of their company, Lord Chamberlain's Men, to become shareholders. Shakespeare thus became a part-owner of the Globe, entitled to ten per cent of the profits. He enjoyed the unique privilege of being a dramatist, actor and businessman.

During the period 1597-99 six more plays comprising comedies and plays on English history were produced:
Merry Wives of Windsor, Much Ado About Nothing, As You Like It, Henry IV-Part One, Henry IV-Part Two, and *Henry V*, probably *Julius Caesar* also had its first staging in 1599.

The new century opened with a personal tragedy to Shakespeare: his father died in 1601. It also brought him to the threshold of his tragic vision—the truest and profoundest ever presented to theatre audiences and to the readers of the world. Before the death of Queen Elizabeth in 1603, the greatest tragedy of personal dilemma *Hamlet* had its first performance. His finest comedy, *Twelfth Night* and the 'problem play' *Troilus and Cressida* were also produced before 1603. With the accession of King James to the English throne, Lord Chamberlain's Men, evidently regarded as the best company of actors, was taken under royal patronage and was renamed King's Men. The letters patent issued on 19 May 1603 mention William Shakespeare along with some other members of the company including Heminge and Condell, the future editors of the first edition of his Collected Plays. The actors of the company became eligible to special privileges; records indicate that they were often called upon to present plays before the Court and to participate in royal pageants and processions—several Shakespeare plays were performed at the Court. In March 1604, when King James made a 'royal proceeding' through the city of London, Shakespeare—as well as each of his fellow players—was given four yards of red cloth for his livery.

On the plane of worldly affairs too, Shakespeare was faring very well. In may 1602 he purchased one hundred and seven acres of arable land to the parish of old Stratford and in September he acquired a cottage in Chapel Lane, Stratford-on-Avon. A fellow actor, Augustine Phillipps, when he made his will in May 1605, mentioned Shakespeare first among the recipients of his bequests of gold pieces: "I give and bequeath to my fellow, William Shakespeare, a thirty-shilling piece in gold." Two years later in 1607 his favourite daughter Susanna, married the physician John Hall and in February 1608 their daughter Elizabeth was born. It is almost certain that Edmond Shakespeare whose burial is recorded in the registers of the Church of St. Saviours in Southwark was the poet's brother. Shakespeare's mother died in 1608.

In Shakespeare's literary output, the period 1604-1608 is the period of great tragedies: *Othello, Macbeth, King Lear, Antony and Cleopatra* and *Cariolanus*. The other plays first produced during this period are: *Measure for Measure, All is Well That Ends Well* and *Timon of Athens*. Some scholars, however, believe that *All's Well That Ends Well* is an early play, perhaps *Love's Labour's Won*, mentioned by Francis Meres in his *Palladis Tamia* (1598).

In 1608 the King's Men took over the Blackfriars, an indoor theatre where Henry Evans's children's company had been staging plays since 1600. Shakespeare thus began writing plays for both Blackfriars and the Globe. He appears to have adjusted himself to the conditions and upper-class audiences at the Blackfriars. Otherwise, too, Shakespeare about this time had emerged from the Inferno of human and supernatural evil. He had explored the genesis, nature, working and consequences of evil and expressed them in the best of utterance. Now in the last phase of his career, he turned to superior kinds of solutions. Evil keeps raising its head, but it is confronted by higher human nature and is overthrown without waste or destruction. This is the tenor of his last plays: *Pericles, Cymbeline, The Winter's Tale, The Tempest*.

William Shakespeare had made his life a grand success: Whatever wrongs, malice, envy or injury he had suffered were behind him; he had become rich and respected; thousands of human hearts had been moved to laughter and tears by the magic of his lines; he had learnt the last lesson in human wisdom.

Around 1611 Shakespeare contentedly retired to Stratford. His remaining two younger brothers, Gilbert and Richard died in 1612 and 1613 respectively. John Combe, one of his closest friends also died in 1613 leaving him a bequest of £ 5. On March 10, 1613, he bought the Blackfriar's Gate House.

Shakespeare did not break his relations completely with his company; he also kept visiting London from time to time. The last two plays which he wrote in collaboration with John Fletcher are *Henry VII* and *The Two Noble Kinsmen*, but his heart wasn't there; they suffer in execution and in imaginative power. Shakespeare's health began to deteriorate after 1613. According to one report some time in 1616 Drayton and Ben Jonson came down to visit him and they had a merry meeting. His will was drawn up in January 1616. Since his younger daughter Judith got married to Thomas Quiney on February 10, the will was revised and executed by him on March 25.

In his will, Shakespeare bequeathed nearly all his property to his elder daughter Susanna Hall and her husband; Judith his younger daughter received very little in comparison. Perhaps Shakespeare was not happy with Judith's marriage to Thomas Quiney about whom there was some scandal, or, he feared any fixed assets made over to her would not remain secure, but he made provision for yearly payment of some money to her. This apparent lack of balance on the part of Shakespeare is bound to remind us of his own creation *King Lear*.

Another matter which causes surprise is the bequest to his wife. She is not mentioned by name and Shakespeare appears to have added one sentence about her as an after thought: "I give unto my wife my second best bed with the furniture". Those who defend Shakespeare on this issue argue that the best bed in the house would be reserved for guests, that he gave her the second best bed because it carried past associations since this must have been the bed the couple used to sleep in. It is also true that Anne's dower rights already stood protected bylaw; she must have continued to live in New Place until her death in 1623. And yet, when all this has been said, one cannot help feeling that this slighting gesture on the part of Shakespeare indicates that something had gone sour in their relations.

He left something to each of his relations: niece Elizabeth Hall, sister Joan and her three sons; he did not forget his friends and the poor of Stratford, to whom he bequeathed ten pounds. It is to be noted that he gave 26s. 8d. each to his former fellow actors, John Heminge, Richard Burbage and Henry Condell for buying mourning rings.

Shakespeare died on 23 April, 1616, but Death could not be proud of this, for in black ink his name still shines bright. A monument representing the poet in the act of writing with a quill was installed some time between his death and the year 1623. This is the famous bust with which the whole world has become familiar. The other authentic likeness is Martin Droeshout's engraving on the title page of the First Folio Collection of Shakespeare's Plays, which is equally familiar to readers. The epitaph inscribed under the bust praises Shakespeare as a writer.

With whome
Quick nature died; whose name doth deck
this tombe
Far more than most, sith all that He hath writt
Leaves living art, but page, to serve his witt.

HAMLET
A CRITICAL INTRODUCTION

No play of Shakespeare's has had a greater hold over readers and spectators and none has given rise to a greater variety of conflicting interpretations than has *Hamlet.* It has been rightly named tragedy of thought, and in this respect, as well as others, takes its place beside *Julius Caeser*. Neither Brutus nor Hamlet is the victim of an over-mastering passion as are the chief persons of the latter tragedies — *e.g., Othello, Macbeth Coriolanus.* The burden of a terrible duty is laid upon each of them, and neither is fitted for bearing such a burden. Brutus is disqualified for action by his moral idealism, his student-like idealism, his capacity for dealing with abstractions rather than with men and things. Hamlet is disqualified for action by his excess of the reflective tendency and by his unstable will, which alternates between complete inactivity and fits of excited energy. Naturally sensitive, he receives a painful shock from the hasty marriage of his mother; already the springs of faith and joy in his nature are embittered; then follows the terrible discovery of his father's murder, with the injunction laid upon him to revenge the crime; upon this again follow the repulses which he receives from Ophelia. A deep melancholy lays hold of his spirit, and all of life grows dark and sad to his vision. Although hating his father's murderer, he has little heart to push on his revenge. He is aware that he is suspected and surrounded by spies. Partly to baffle them, partly to create a veil behind which to seclude his true self, partly because his whole moral nature is indeed deeply disordered, he assumes the part of one whose wits have gone astray. Except for one loyal friend, he is alone among enemies or supposed traitors. Ophelia he regards as no more loyal or honest to him than his mother had been to her dead husband. The ascertainment of Claudius's guilt by means of the play still leaves him incapable of the last decisive act of vengeance. Not so, however, with the king, who now, recognizing his foe in Hamlet, does not delay to despatch him to a bloody death in England. But there is in Hamlet a terrible power of sudden and desperate action. From the melancholy which broods over him after the burial of Ophelia, he rouses himself to the play of swords with Laertes, and at last, with strength which leaps up before its final extinction, he accomplishes the punishment of the malefactor. Horatio, with his fortitude, his self-possession, his strong equanimity is a contrast to the prince. And Laertes, who takes violent measures at the shortest notice to avenge his father's murder, is in another way a contrast; but Laertes is the young gallant of the period, and his capacity for action arises in part from the absence of those moral checks of which Hamlet is sensible. Polonius is owner of the shallow wisdom of this world, and exhibits this grotesquely while now on the brink of dotage; he sees, but cannot see through Hamlet's ironical mockery of him. Ophelia is tender, sensitive, affectionate, but the reverse of heroic; she fails Hamlet in his need, and then in her turn becoming the sufferer, gives way under the pressure of her afflictions. We do not honour, we only commiserate her.

(i) THE DEVELOPMENT OF THE PLOT OF THE PLAY

Act I; Scene (i): Hamlet's friend, Horatio, meets the two officers, Marcellus and Bernardo, on the ramparts of the castle of Elsinore, to test the truth of their story of the ghost of Hamlet's father appearing there. As Bernardo is relating the story, the ghost appears again. It is undoubtedly the late king in full armour. Soon it disappears. The dawn is approaching and Horatio rushes to apprise Hamlet of the ominous developments.

Act I; Scene (ii): Claudius holds his court with Polonius, the Lord Chamberlaine. Claudius is especially warm towards his nephew, Hamlet but Hamlet is cold and aloof. The Queen intervenes to ask him to drop his idea of returning to the University of Wittenburg, which Hamlet reluctantly agrees to do. As Hamlet leaves, he meets Horatio and the guards who tell him of the ghost's appearance. He is very much disturbed and wants to see the ghost himself. He administers Horatio and the guards a solemn oath never to talk about the ghost.

Act I; Scene (iii): Polonius's son, Laertes is going back to Paris. He gives parting instructions to his sister, Ophelia, to avoid Hamlet's company for Hamlet's intentions he doubts very much. Polonius also warns Ophelia likewise. Ophelia meekly submits herself to their warnings.

Act I; Scene (iv): Hamlet and Horatio join the guards around midnight and await the ghost's appearance. As it appears, Hamlet is profoundly shocked at first. Later he regains his objectivity a bit. The ghost beckons Hamlet to follow it. Hamlet goes ahead, ignoring all warnings. He threatens violence, if he is held black.

Act I; Scene (v): The ghost takes Hamlet to a lonely place and there it discloses that Claudius had killed him by pouring poison in his ears as he was sleeping in the orchard one afternoon. Then Claudius had seduced his "most seeming virtuous-queen" to agree to marry him. As the ghost disappears Hamlet returns to his friend and warns him and the guards never to betray the happenings to anybody.

Act II; Scene (i): Polonius sends some letters and money to his son, Laertes in Paris through his servant, Reynaldo, instructing him to spy on Laertes's activities there.

Ophelia appears in a highly distraught condition and tells Polonius how Hamlet had come to her in a disordered attire and had behaved in a strange manner. Polonius immediately jumps to the conclusion that an unhappy love affair has temporarily affected Hamlet's reason, for Ophelia, under his instructions, has not responded to his pleas of love. He decides to report all this to the king, Claudius.

Act II; Scene (ii): The king and the queen are anxious to find the cause of Hamlet's deranged conduct. They entrust this to Hamlet's fellow students, Rosencrantz and Guildenstern who are to spy on Hamlet. As they leave, Polonius appears and informs the king of the successful accomplishment of the assignment of the court ambassadors who had gone to protest to the king of Norway against the hostile activities of the young Fortinbras. Then he informs the king of his view that failure in love has made Hamlet mad. He also shows the king a letter from Hamlet to Ophelia begging credence for his love. Polonius says that he can arrange a meeting between Hamlet and Ophelia, as if by chance, where he will play the eavesdropper alongwith the king. Just then Hamlet enters, reading a book. Polonius urges all others to leave him alone with Hamlet. He then asks Hamlet if he knows him. Hamlet plays a madman with Polonius and asks him to protect his daughter from all external contact to avoid an unwanted pregnancy. Just then Rosencrantz and Guildenstern come. Hamlet greets them warmly but soon relapses to his melancholy mood. He tells them he finds no delight anywhere. His friends assure him that a troupe of players, which awaits him, will certainly delight him. As the players enter, Hamlet draws one of them aside and asks him to arrange the enactment of the play, *The*

Murder of Gonzago, the next night. He tells him that he would insert a self-composed speech in it for them to read out. All others leave and Hamlet bemoans the fact that he has done nothing so far to avenge the murder of his father. But he assures himself that he would test the veracity of the ghost's account by subjecting his uncle to a psychological test. He calls the play to be enacted a 'mouse trap' for it would re-enact the manner in which his father was murdered.

Act III; Scene (i): Rosencrantz and Guildenstern report to Claudius their failure with Hamlet. Claudius asks them to keep trying. Polonius goes ahead with his plan to arrange a meeting between Hamlet and Ophelia. Ophelia is told her part. Hamlet enters debating the relative value of life and death. He sees Ophelia engaged in reading a book. He greets her warmly but she begs him to take back all his love-presents for he is changed now. Hamlet reverts to his melancholy. He treats her as a stranger, advising her to cling to her virtue for the world is corrupt. Hamlet leaves and Ophelia weeps for the change in the once-so-perfect, Hamlet. However, Claudius rejects Polonius's theory. He suspects that Hamlet has something in his soul which he broods over. Polonius, nevertheless, wants another test. He proposes that a meeting between Hamlet and his mother be arranged and he himself would overhear the talk. The king agrees.

Act III; Scene (ii): Hamlet joins the players in a hall where they are getting ready for enacting a play. Hamlet behaves normally with them. Then he calls Horatio whom he asks to observe Claudius during the enactment. He would decide his further course of action by the outcome of this plan of his. The play begins with a dumb show. A king and a queen come on the stage and exchange vows of eternal love. The king lies down to sleep and the queen leaves. Enters a person who pours poison in the king's ears. The queen enters again, finds the king dead and makes a passionate show of lamentations. The poisoner returns, woos the queen with gifts. After initial unwillingness, the queen accepts his love and the two walk away hand-in-hand. The King, Claudius, abruptly orders the players to stop the show and leaves the hall. Hamlet now seems convinced of the ghost's account.

Act III; Scene (iii): Claudius orders Rosencrantz and Guildenstern to conduct Hamlet to England with secret instructions to the English King to execute Hamlet as soon as he lands there. As he bends down in prayer with a troubled conscience, Hamlet, on his way to meet the Queen, passes by Claudius's side, unnoticed. Hamlet thinks it is a golden opportunity to kill his enemy but by doing so now, he would only send his enemy's soul to Heaven and therefore, he desists.

Act III; Scene (iv): As Hamlet goes to the Queen's chamber, Polonius hides himself behind the arras. The queen reprimands Hamlet for offending his stepfather by his behaviour. Hamlet retorts that it is she who has offended his father by being instrumental in his murder and by marrying the murderer later. The queen cries for help as Hamlet thrusts her into a chair to stop her from leaving. Polonius moves behind the arras and impulsively Hamlet thrusts his sword, through the arras, killing Polonius. Hamlet's overwhelming rage bursts out. He shouts that he is but mad in craft and ordains her never to share her bed with Claudius. He tells her that Claudius is dispatching him to England with Rosencrantz and Guildenstern. Then he leaves, dragging Polonius's body with him.

Act IV; Scene (i): The Queen hastens to the King to tell him how Hamlet is 'mad as the sea and wind', for he thrust his rapier through the arras and killed Polonaius. The king feels alarmed.

Act IV; Scene (ii): Rosencrantz and Guildenstern meet] Hamlet and try to find out where he had hidden Polonius's body. Hamlet asks them to take him to the King.

Act IV; Scene (iii): The King asks Hamlet where he has hidden Polonius's body. Hamlet continues to feign madness. In a soliloquy, the King reveals his secret plan. He is arranging the execution of Hamlet in England.

Act IV; Scene (iv): As Hamlet sets forth to go to England, he encounters Fortinbras, on his way to Poland to fight a war for honour's sake. Hamlet is full of self-reproach for his 'inaction'.

Act IV; Scene (v): Polonius's death turns Ophelia's wits and she appears in inconsolable grief. Laertes returns to Claudius's court with a drawn sword in hand, but he is pacified by the King.

Act IV; Scene (vi): Horatio receives a letter from Hamlet informing him of the attack on his ship, and his being taken prisoner. Rosencrantz and Guildenstern have proceeded to England. Horatio is required to see Hamlet as instructed by him.

Act IV; Scene (vii): Claudius and Laertes are in secret consultations. A letter from Hamlet is delivered to the King. Claudius feels alarmed to discover Hamlet in Denmark. He unfolds his plan to Laertes. He will arrange a contest of fencing between Hamlet and Laertes. Laertes will be given a deadly weapon with which he can kill Hamlet. To be absolutely sure, Laertes plans to put a deadly poison on its point. The gratified Claudius puts the crowning touch to the plan by announcing that he'll have a cup of poison ready for Hamlet, in any case.

Act V; Scene (i): A grave is being dug for somebody who has committed suicide. Hamlet reflects on the futility of human life and ambitions. Hamlet now discovers that it is Ophelia who is to be buried here. Laertes, in sorrow, leaps into the grave and demands to be buried with Ophelia. Hamlet too follows him there and claims that his love for Ophelia was much greater than Laertes's. The two fight but are separated.

Act V; Scene (ii): Hamlet learns of the fencing match between him and Laertes. The king, the queen and all courtiers gather to witness the match. Laertes carries a poison-touched sword and Claudius readies a cup of poison for Hamlet, to be offered after the match. At the very outset Hamlet apologizes to Laertes for killing Polonius in a fit of madness. The fight begins. Hamlet scores three hits over Laertes. The overjoyed Queen drinks the cup of poisoned wine in celebration. Laertes also scratches Hamlet with the poisoned end. The queen falls down crying that she has been poisoned. Laertes is also dying. He reveals Claudius's game plan. Hamlet, himself nearing the end, wounds the king with the same poisoned rapier. He also pours forcibly the remaining draught of the poisoned drink into the mouth of the king. Laertes and the king die immediately. Hamlet gives a parting message to Horatio and then dies. According to Hamlet's wishes, Fortinbras is made the King of Denmark and Horatio takes upon himself the task of explaining the whole situation to his countrymen.

(ii) THE PLAY WITHIN THE PLAY

The play within the play constitutes an important part of *Hamlet.* A distinction must be made here between the story of the play and its plot. The plot of *Hamlet* begins with the appearance of the Ghost. But the story begins with the poisoning of his brother by Claudius to obtain the crown and the love of Gertrude. Thus, the inner play marks the dramatisation of the beginning of the story for the audience. The actual act of poisoning is performed twice, once in the dumb show preceding the play and once with words as well as gestures. Shakespeare has used a dumb show for the same reason that he has used an inner play. The dumb show concerns the murder that is past — the murder of a king by an unknown hand. The rest of the play shows an image of the murder that is yet to come — the murder of a king by the aggrieved nephew. Hamlet significantly enough exclaims for the benefit of Claudius, introducing the murderer, "This is one Lucianus, nephew to the king."

There are other important questions, posed in the play by this juxtaposition. If Hamlet were to complete the act of revenge and kill his uncle, he would find himself playing the part of Lucianus, i.e., he would be a secret murderer by poison like Claudius. Murder should be revenged but is revenge also not murder? How can one act against Claudius without copying Claudius? The inner play, which dramatises this seemingly insoluble problem, also provides its resolution. Claudius had won Gertrude with the witchcraft of his wits and by poisoning his brother's ear. He himself is now poisoned through his ear, the poison here is the witchcraft of words spoken by an actor on a stage. At one level it does seem ironical that *The Murder of Gonzago* is really a successful act of vengeance against the king by Hamlet.

There are other important aspects of the play within the play. On either side of the inner play Shakespeare places a conversation about music between Hamlet and Horatio, and Hamlet and Rosencrantz and Guildenstern. Music obviously is a Renaissance symbol of the proper harmony of the entire universe. Horatio, with all his elements in proper balance, is not a pipe to be played on by Fortune. Rosencrantz and Guildenstern, on the other hand, seek to play on Hamlet as a pipe, even as the audience itself is made to examine the nature of Hamlet's own harmony and balance of soul.

The questions of balance and harmony are also posed tentalizingly in the two great soliloquies which also appear on either side of the inner play. Before this play, Hamlet bitterly compares his own conduct to that of the actor who was prepared to weep at the sorrows of Hecuba, underlining his own pitifully inadequate reaction. After the inner play Hamlet's soliloquy is motivated by his encounter with the army of Fortinbras; the soldiers are risking their lives for a 'straw', whereas, he has a father treacherously wronged. But the fact of the matter is that between these two lamentations, Hamlet has acted and acted through the inner play which catches the conscience of the king, as Hamlet had planned. Besides, it warns Claudius of the danger and thus, the inner play becomes the pivot round which the play, *Hamlet,* comes to revolve.

Last but not least, the inner play holds a mirror image of death up to Hamlet. Although the nature of the act of vengeance is one of the central questions in the play as such, Hamlet himself is never made to doubt or question his duty to avenge his father's murder. It is important to notice that to believe Hamlet's condemnation of his own actions is to assume that he ought, instantly, to have taken violent measures against the king. The inner play poses this stark truth in its most pointed form.

(iii) THE ROLE OF HAMLET

In Hamlet's soliloquies and actions of the play, Shakespeare dramatizes the considerations of conscience and the power of thought which prevent Hamlet, literally against his will, from achieving his desired blood revenge. Hamlet's troubled mind is the deliberate creation of Shakespeare's and he has presented it to his audience with a great deal of conscious artistic skill. In the course of the play Hamlet has seven long soliloquies. The first of these (Act I; Scene 2; lines 129-59) occurs before he has scene the Ghost. The second (Act I, Scene 5, lines 92-112) appears immediately after it has told its story of incest adultery. Both the speeches are concerned with memory. The next two soliloquies are concerned with through or 'conscience'. The third (Act II; Scene 2; lines 557-616 is spoken after the player's recitation and is concerned with the power of thought which makes the actor pause for pity. It ends with the decision to 'catch the king's conscience'. The fourth is 'To be, or not to be...' (Act III; Scene 1; lines 56-90) where thought faces the fact of death and conscience is said to make us cowards by restraining us from suicide. The fifth and the sixth soliloquies are concerned with blood and will; one (Act III; Scene 2, lines 395-406) is spoken on his way to his mother's private apartments, the other (Act III; Scene 3; lines 73-96), the 'damnation soliloquy' perhaps at the back of the apparently kneeling-in-prayer king. St. Augustine had described the three powers of the soul as Memory, Understanding and Will. These six soliloquies dramatise exactly these powers in Hamlet's soul and show how his memory and understanding are irrevocably opposed to his will. A part of Hamlet desires to play the part of Lucianus and kill the king but he is prevented by the stronger, though unconscious, forces of his memory and conscience.

The last soliloquy (Act IV; Scene 4; lines 32-66) is concerned with all three powers of the soul. In the end the play shows us three sons, all faced with the task of avenging their fathers and defining at the same time their own place in the world. Fortinbras takes the traditional course of attempting to reassert his rights by force of arms. It is on his return from his campaign of honour in Poland that he appears as a man in full armour, to speak the last lines of the play and remind the audience of the important role that is inevitably played in human affairs by force of arms and the virtues of the active life. Laertes, on the other hand, is more a representative of the passionate life. His memory of his father causes him to cast aside all restrains of law or conscience.

His attitude to Hamlet is that he is prepared, to 'cut his throat i' th' church'. It is impossible not to sympathise with this attitude but Shakespeare also takes care to let his audience see that it is self-destructive as well as horrible. In breaking every law and custom of honour and courtesy in order to kill Hamlet, Laertes also devises the method of his own death.

Hamlet follows an altogether different course of action. In the first place, he pauses for thought — the only time that he does not do so, he kills Polonius and thus, himself becomes a victim of vengeance as well as an avenger. Three times in the play he acts and each time his action is an appeal to the conscience of another character. He troubles the king's conscience when he acts out through the staging of the inner play and Claudius retaliates by repeating his crime. Hamlet successfully arouses the Queen's conscience in the closet scene. Finally, he appeals to the conscience of Laertes immediately before the duel with the poisoned sword. With Claudius, Hamlet fails but with both the Queen and Laertes he does succeed. The Queen's moving away from the king's side to that of her son in the duel scene is one of the most terrible scenes in the play. She comes out to wipe the sweat from Hamlet's forehead. Even as the king attempts to stop her, she lifts the cup of the poisoned drink to her lips to carouse to the son's fortunes. Even the appeal to the implacable avenger in Laertes finds its mark, though not until both Hamlet and Laertes are dying. The forgiveness and mutual charity which Hamlet and Laertes then exchange is the only way in which the long cycle of revenge can be broken and men can live in harmony and love within the sacred eternal dance of the Graces.

Hamlet is certainly not a perfect character. One may understand his depression and melancholy but he does fail to appreciate the worth of Ophelia as well as the Queen. He kills Polonius by mistake, but it is with clear calculation that he sends both Rosencrantz and Guildenstern to their deaths. Nevertheless, throughout the pattern of deaths by poison, the constant playing of deceitful parts and the duel of impassioned words and poisoned rapiers, it is Hamlet who by constant questions, continually draws the attention of the audience to the possibility of the existence of values like honour, conscience and love. It is Hamlet's insistence that even the part of death, which is unavoidable and inevitable, be faced with courage, good humour and understanding. It is this, in the final analysis, that distinguishes Hamlet from the other characters and makes *Hamlet* his tragedy even though a number of others meet a similar fate.

(iv) OTHER CHARACTERS IN THE PLAY

(a) Polonius

Polonius is a blundering, blithering fool, though he thinks himself to be a very wise and astute politician. Devoid of any scruple of conscience or a nice sense of humour, he can stoop to anything to accomplish his ends. He is apt for vile and crooked means only. He sends Reynaldo to spy on his son in Paris. The practical wisdom he loads Laertes with can descend to low and mean tricks. His handling of Ophelia betrays a coarse and filthy mind. Even the manner of his death suits him well. He goes after Hamlet to the Queen's chamber : "Behind the arras I'll convey myself/To hear the process." And it is a sword-thrust, meant for his master that undoes him. An inglorious life meeting an inglorious death.

(b) Laertes

Laertes looks a slightly more sagacious and shrewder Polonius in the making. Polonius-like he lectures Ophelia who questions his own conduct, revealing only his immaturity. The ease with which Claudius disarms his anger at Polonius's death again reveals his naivety. The nefarious plot he enters into with Claudius to hit Hamlet with a poison-touched sword again shows his unscruplousness. It is only when he himself is hit by his own venomed sword that he confesses "1 am justly kill'd with my own treachery". Laertes with his easy morality, which he can preach so well to his sister, becomes a ready instrument of the king's villainy but he does have the grace to confess his crime.

(c) Claudius

Claudius is obviously the villain of the piece. He murders Hamlet's father, seduces his mother and ascends the throne to the exclusion of Hamlet. Hamlet speaks contemptuously of him — his father is Hyperion and Claudius is a satyr. But we find him behaving with dignity and statesman-like wisdom when he presides at the Council. Claudius is shrewd while Polonius is fatuous. He keeps a placid exterior and extraordinary self-possession. When he is at prayer and Hamlet passes by and spares him, we have a glimpse into his inner being. After all he is not yet a seasoned villain, though possessing all the art and accomplishment of a villain :

"O, my offence is rank, it smells to heaven.
It hath the primal eldest upon 't,
A brother's murder."

But he gets more and more seasoned in his villainy. When he finds his security shattered by the sudden tidings of the failure of his plot against Hamlet, the roused devil in him turns on the instant to make Laertes his accomplice in another plot. But his conspiracy to have Hamlet poisoned to death in a fencing duel with Laertes recoils on him and lie meets an unheroic death.

(d) Ophelia

Ophelia strikes one as passive, non-resisting even to the extent of being unwilling party to conspiracies against Hamlet whom she professes to love. She is used as a decoy by the King and Polonius. Hamlet sees through it all and this makes him sceptical of Ophelia's protestations of love, even cynical, a misogynist. She may not answer Hamlet's exacting standard of Honour and she may be unaware of the dishonourableness of her part in playing the spy upon Hamlet. It may be partly explained by the vile court atmosphere as well as her home atmosphere which must have tainted her. She, in the final analysis, seems to have no individuality of her own and the meddling of her father, her brother, the king and even the queen in her private affairs brings on her suffering and a tragic fate. It is, doubtful whether any character in Shakespeare is more completely a victim to the requirement of tragedy.

(v) THE PSYCHO-ANALYTIC SOLUTION TO THE PROBLEMS IN HAMLET

Dr. Ernst Jones turns to psychology to tackle the enigma that *Hamlet* seems to have become for the critics : why does Hamlet delay his revenge; whether he is really mad or just posing to be mad; whether *Hamlet* constitutes an artistic success or failure and so on. Dr. Jones considers the opinion of a number of distinguished critics before he pronounces his judgement. Ulrici in 1839 put forth the view that Hamlet gravely doubted the moral legitimacy of revenge. There was thus a struggle between his natural tendency to avenge his father and his highly developed ethical and Christian views. Stoll suggested that the conflict was a purely intellectual one, rather than being a moral conflict. Hamlet was just unable to satisfy himself of the adequacy or reliability of the Ghost's evidence. But then, why did Hamlet in his monologues give us no indication whatsoever of the nature of the conflict in his mind? He gave several pretended excuses for his hesitancy, but never once did he hint at any doubt about what his duty was in the matter. Throughout the play we see his mind irrevocably made up on the desirability of a given course of action, which he fully accepts as being his bounden duty. Dr. Jones detects Hamlet's confession of his nonconsciousness of the cause of his repugnance to the task. In his bitter cry in Act IV, Scene 3, "I do not know why..." he reveals us to himself in so many words. If it had only been a question of conflict between the duty of revenge imposed from without and an inner moral or juristic counter-impulse, this discord and its cause must have been brought into the region of thought in such a reflective person as Hamlet. The only conclusion, thus, is that Hamlet's hesitancy was due to some special cause of repugnance for his task and that he himself was unaware of the nature of this repugnance.

Loening has objected to this hypothesis that there is some hidden cause agitating Hamlet's mind. He asks : why has the poet not put in a clearer light the mental trend we are trying to discover? Perhaps it is with this impression in mind that T.S. Eliot opined that Hamlet's emotion is in excess of the facts as they appear. But if the motive of the play is so obscure, to what can we attribute its powerful impact on the audience? Clearly the hero and the audience are all profoundly moved by feelings due to a conflict of the source of which they are unaware. Psychoanalysis alone can help untangle this mystery. Hamlet's advocates say he cannot do his duty, his detractors say he will not, whereas, the truth is that he cannot will. The grounds Hamlet gives for his hesitancy are grounds none of which will stand any serious consideration, and which continually change from one time to another. One moment he pretends he is too cowardly to perform the deed, at another he questions the truthfulness of the ghost, at another—when the opportunity presents itself in its naked form—he thinks the time is unsuited, it would be better to wait till the king was at some evil act and then to kill him, and so on. Nevertheless, it is noticeable how his outbursts of remorse are evoked by external happenings which bring back to his mind his resolve for revenge; particularly effective in this respect are incidents that contrast with his own conduct, as when the player is so moved over the fate of Hecuba (Act II, Scene 2), or when Fortinbras takes the field and "finds quarrel in a straw when honour's at the stake" (Act IV; Scene 4).

The whole picture presented by Hamlet, his deep depression, the hopeless note in his attitude towards the world and towards the value of life, his dread of death, his repeated reference to bad dreams, his self-accusations, his desperate efforts to get away from the thoughts of his duty, and his vain attempts to find an excuse for his procrastination — all this unequivocally points to some hidden ground for shirking his task, a ground which he dare not or cannot avow to himself. The psychoanalytic cause for Hamlet's otherwise inexplicable behaviour is the reactivization of his early wish in the death of his father (for he considered his father his rival in his love for his mother) at the hands of Claudius. As a child he had the wish but he had got over it by piety and other educative influences but now it reasserts itself and produces the very symptoms Hamlet is described as having.

The Tragedy of Hamlet, Prince of Denmark

THE ACTORS' NAMES

CLAUDIUS, King of Denmark
HAMLET, son to the late, and nephew to the present King
POLONIUS, Lord Chamberlain
HORATIO, friend to Hamlet
LAERTES, son of Polonius
VOLTEMAND, CORNELIUS, ROSENCRANTZ, GUILDENSTERN, OSRIC, A GENTLEMAN, — courtiers
A PRIEST
MARCELLUS, BERNARDO, FRANCISCO, — soldiers
REYNALDO, servant to Polonius
The Players
Two Clowns, grave-diggers
FORTINBRAS, Prince of Norway
A Captain
English Ambassadors
GERTRUDE, Queen of Denmark, and mother to Hamlet
OPHELIA, daughter to Polonius
GHOST of Hamlet's Father

I.1

Enter Bernardo and Francisco, two sentinels.

BERNARDO: Who's there?
FRANCISCO: Nay answer me. Stand and unfold yourself.
BERNARDO: Long live the King.
FRANCISCO: Bernardo?
BERNARDO: He.
FRANCISCO: You come most carefully upon your hour.
BERNARDO: 'Tis now struck twelve, get thee to bed Francisco.
FRANCISCO: For this relief much thanks: 'tis bitter cold, And I am sick at heart.
BERNARDO: Have you had quiet guard?
FRANCISCO: Not a mouse stirring.
BERNARDO: Well, good night.
If you do meet Horatio and Marcellus,
The rivals of my watch, bid them make haste.

Enter Horatio and Marcellus.

FRANCISCO: I think I hear them. Stand: ho, who is there?
HORATIO: Friends to this ground.
MARCELLUS: And liegemen to the Dane.
FRANCISCO: Give you good night.
MARCELLUS: O, farewell honest soldiers, who hath reliev'd you?
FRANCISCO: Bernardo has my place: give you good night.

Exit Francisco.

MARCELLUS: Holla Bernardo.
BERNARDO: Say, what is Horatio there?

HORATIO: A piece of him.
BERNARDO: Welcome Horatio, welcome good Marcellus.
MARCELLUS: What, has this thing appear'd again to-night?
BERNARDO: I have seen nothing.
MARCELLUS: Horatio says, 'tis but our fantasy,
And will not let belief take hold of him
Touching this dreaded sight, twice seen of us;
Therefore I have entreated him along
With us, to watch the minutes of this night,
That if again this apparition come,
He may approve our eyes, and speak to it.
HORATIO: Tush, tush, 'twill not appear.
BERNARDO: Sit down awhile,
And let us once again assail your ears,
That are so fortified against our story,
What we two nights have seen.
HORATIO: Well, sit we down,
And let us hear Bernardo speak of this.
BERNARDO: Last night of all,
When yond same star that's westward from the pole
Had made his course t' illume that part of heaven
Where now it burns, Marcellus and myself,
The bell then beating one–
MARCELLUS: Peace, break thee off:

Enter Ghost.

Look where it comes again.
BERNARDO: In the same figure, like the King that's dead.
MARCELLUS: Thou art a scholar, speak to it Horatio.
BERNARDO: Looks it not like the King? Mark it Horatio.
HORATIO: Most like: it harrows me with fear and wonder.
BERNARDO: It would be spoke to.
MARCELLUS: Question it Horatio.
HORATIO: What art thou that usurp'st this time of night,

Together with that fair and warlike form
In which the Majesty of buried Denmark
Did sometimes march: by heaven I charge thee speak.
MARCELLUS: It is offended.
BERNARDO: See, it stalks away.
HORATIO: Stay, speak; speak: I charge thee, speak.

Exit the Ghost.

MARCELLUS: 'Tis gone, and will not answer.
BERNARDO: How now Horatio? you tremble and look pale:
Is not this something more than fantasy?
What think you on't?
HORATIO: Before my God, I might not this believe
Without the sensible and true avouch
Of mine own eyes.
MARCELLUS: Is it not like the King?
HORATIO: As thou art to thyself,
Such was the very armour he had on,
When he th' ambitious Norway combated:
So frown'd he once, when in an angry parle
He smote the sledded poleaxe on the ice.
'Tis strange.
MARCELLUS: Thus twice before, and jump at this dead hour,
With martial stalk, hath he gone by our watch.
HORATIO: In what particular thought to work, I know not:
But in the gross and scope of my opinion,
This bodes some strange eruption to our State.
MARCELLUS: Good now sit down, and tell me he that knows
Why this same strict and most observant watch,
So nightly toils the subject of the land,
And why such daily cast of brazen cannon
And foreign mart for implements of war:
Why such impress of shipwrights, whose sore task
Does not divide be Sunday from the week,

What might be toward, that this sweaty haste
Doth make the night joint-labourer with the day:
Who is't that can inform met?

HORATIO: That can I,
At least the whisper goes so: our last King,
Whose image even but now appear'd to us,
Was (as you know) by Fortinbras of Norway,
(Thereto prick'd on by a most emulate pride)
Dar'd to the combat. In which, our valiant Hamlet,
(For so this side of our known world esteem'd him)
Did slay this Fortinbras: who by a seal'd compact,
Well ratified by law, and heraldry,
Did forfeit (with his life) all those his lands
Which he stood siez'd of, to the conqueror:
Against the which, a moiety competent
Was gaged by our King: which had return'd
To the inheritance of Fortinbras,
Had he been vanquisher, as by the same cov'nant
And carriage of the article design'd ,
His fell to Hamlet. Now sir, young Fortinbras,
Of unimproved mettle, hot and full
Hath in the skirts of Norway, here and there,
Shark'd up a list of landless resolutes,
For food and diet, to some enterprise
That hath a stomach in't: which is no other
(As it doth well appear unto our state)
But to recover of us by strong hand
And terms compulsative, those foresaid lands
So by his father lost: and this (I take it)
Is the main motive of our preparations,
The source of this our watch, and the chief head
Of this post haste, and romage in the land.

[BERNARDO; I think it be no other, but e'en so;
Well may it sort that this portentous figure
Comes armed through our watch so like the King
That was and is the question of these wars.

HORATIO: A moth it is to trouble the mind's eye:
In the most high and palmy state of Rome,
A little ere the mightiest Julius fell,
The graves stood tenantless, and the sheeted dead
Did squeak and gibber in the Roman streets;
As stars with trains of fire and dews of blood,
Disasters in the sun; and the moist star,
Upon whose influence Neptune's empire stands,
Was sick almost to doomsday with eclipse.
And even the like precurse of fierce events,
As harbingers preceding still the fates
And prologue to the omen coming on,
Have heaven and earth together demonstrated
Unto our climatures and countrymen.]

Enter Ghost again.

But soft, behold: lo, where it comes again:
I'll cross it, though it blast me. Stay illusion:

Ghost spreads his arms.

If thou hast any sound, or use of voice,
Speak to me.
If there be any good thing to be done,
That may to thee do ease, and grace to me:
Speak to me.
If thou art privy to thy country's fate
(Which happily foreknowing may avoid)
O speak.
Or, if thou hast uphoarded in thy life
Extorted treasure in the womb of earth,
(For which, they say, you spirits oft walk in death)

The Cock crows.

Speak of it. Stay, and speak. Stop it Marcellus.
MARCELLUS: Shall I strike at it with my partisan?
HORATIO: Do, if it will not stand.

BERNARDO : 'Tis here.
HORATIO: 'Tis here.

Exit Ghost.

MARCELLUS: 'Tis gone.
We do it wrong, being so majestical
To offer it the show of violence,
For it is as the air, invulnerable,
And our vain blows, malicious mockery.
BERNARDO: It was about to speak, when the cock crew.
HORATIO: And then it started, like a guilty thing
Upon a fearful summons. I have heard,
The cock that is the trumpet to the morn,
Doth with his lofty and shrill-sounding throat
Awake the god of day: and at his warning,
Whether in sea, or fire, in earth, or air,
Th' extravagant, and erring spirit, hies
To his confine: and of the truth herein,
This present object made probation.
MARCELLUS: It faded on the crowing of the cock.
Some say, that ever 'gainst that season comes
Wherein our Saviour's birth is celebrated,
The bird of dawning singeth all night long:
And then (they say) no spirit can walk abroad,
The nights are wholesome, then no planets strike,
No fairy takes, nor witch hath power to charm:
So hallow'd, and so gracious is the time.
HORATIO: So have I heard, and do in part believe it.
But look, the morn in russet mantle clad,
Walks o'er the dew of yon high eastern hill;
Break we our watch up, and by my advice
Let us impart what we have seen to-night
Unto young Hamlet. For upon my life,
This spirit dumb to us will speak to him:
Do you consent we shall acquaint him with it,
As needful in our loves, fitting our duty?

MARCELLUS: Let's do't I pray, and I this morning know
Where we shall find him most conveniently.
Exeunt.

I.2

Flourish. Enter Claudius, King of Denmark, Gertrude, the Queen; Council, as Polonius, and his son, Laertes, Hamlet and others.

KING: Though yet of Hamlet our dear brother's death
The memory be green: and that it us befitted
To bear our hearts in grief, and our whole Kingdom
To be contracted in one brow of woe:
Yet so far hath discretion fought with nature,
That we with wisest sorrow think on him,
Together with remembrance of ourselves.
Therefore our sometimes sister, now our Queen,
Th' imperial jointress to this warlike State,
Have we, as 'twere, with a defeated joy,
With one auspicious, and one dropping eye,
With mirth in funeral, and with dirge in marriage,
In equal scale weighing delight and dole
Taken to wife; nor have we herein barr'd
Your better wisdoms, which have freely gone
With this affair along, for all our thanks.
Now follows, that you know young Fortinbras,
Holding a weak supposal of our worth;
Or thinking by our late dear Brother's death
Our State to be disjoint, and out of frame,
Colleagued with the dream of his advantage;

He hath not fail'd to pester us with message,
Importing the surrender of those lands
Lost by his father, with all bonds of law
To our most valiant brother: so much for him.

Enter Voltemand and Cornelius.

Now for ourself, and for this time of meeting,
Thus much the business is. We have here writ
To Norway, uncle of young Fortinbras,
Who impotent and bed-rid, scarcely hears
Of this his nephew's purpose, to suppress
His further gait herein. In that the levies,
The lists, and full proportions are all made
Out of his subject: and we here dispatch
You good Cornelius, and you Voltemand,
For bearing of this greeting to old Norway,
Giving to you no further personal power
To business with the King, more than the scope
Of these dilated articles allow:
Farewell, and let your haste commend your duty.
VOLTEMAND: In that, and all things, will we show our duty.
KING: We doubt it nothing, heartily farewell.

Exeunt Voltemand and Cornelius.

And now Laertes, what's the news with you?
You told us of some suit. What is't Laertes?
You cannot speak of reason to the Dane,
And lose your voice. What wouldst thou beg Laertes,
That shall not be my offer, not thy asking?
The head is not more native to the heart,
The hand more instrumental to the mouth,
Than is the throne of Denmark to thy father.
What wouldst thou have Laertes?

LAERTES: Dread my Lord,
Your leave and favour to return to France.
From whence, though willingly I came to Denmark
To show my duty in your Coronation,
Yet now I must confess, that duty done,
My thoughts and wishes bend again toward France,
And bow them to your gracious leave and pardon.
KING: Have you your father's leave? What says Polonius?
POLONIUS: He hath my Lord, [wrung from me my slow leave
By laboursome petition and at last
Upon his will I seal'd my hard consent;]
I do beseech you give him leave to go.
KING: Take thy fair hour Laertes, time be thine,
And thy best graces spend it at thy will:
But now my cousin Hamlet, and my son?
HAMLET: A little more than kin, and less than kind.
KING: How is it that the clouds still hang on you?
HAMLET: Not so my Lord, I am too much i' th' sun.
QUEEN: Good Hamlet cast thy nightly colour off,
And let thine eye look like a friend on Denmark.
Do not for ever with thy vailed lids
Seek for thy noble father in the dust;
Thou know'st 'tis common, all that lives must die,
Passing through nature, to eternity.
HAMLET: Ay Madam, it is common.
QUEEN: If it be,
Why seems it so particular with thee?
HAMLET: Seems Madam? nay, it is: I know not seems:
'Tis not alone my inky cloak, good mother,
Nor customary suits of solemn black,
Nor windy suspiration of forc'd breath.
No, nor the fruitful river in the eye,
Nor the dejected haviour of the visage,
Together with all forms, moods, shows of grief,
That can denote me truly. These indeed seem,

For they are actions that a man might play:
But I have that within, which passeth show;
These, but the trappings and the suits of woe.
KING: 'Tis sweet and commendable in your nature Hamlet,
To give these mourning duties to your father:
But you must know, your father lost a father,
That father lost, lost his, and the survivor bound
In filial obligation, for some term
To do obsequious sorrow. But to persever
In obstinate condolement, is a course
Of impious stubbornness. 'Tis unmanly grief,
It shows a will most incorrect to Heaven,
A heart unfortified, a mind impatient
An understanding simple, and unschool'd:
For, what we know must be, and is as common
As any the most vulgar thing to sense,
Why should we in our peevish opposition
Take it to heart? Fie, 'tis a fault to Heaven,
A fault against the dead, a fault to nature,
To reason most absurd, whose common theme
Is death of fathers, and who still hath cried,
From the first corse, till he that died to-day,
This must be so. We pray you throw to earth
This unprevailing woe, and think of us
As of a father; for let the world take note,
You are the most immediate to our Throne,
And with no less nobility of love,
Than that which dearest father bears his son,
Do I impart towards you. For your intent
In going back to school in Wittenberg,
It is most retrograde to our desire:
And we beseech you, bend you to remain
Here in the cheer and comfort of our eye,
Our chiefest courtier, cousin, and our son.

QUEEN: Let not thy mother lose her prayers Hamlet:
I prithee stay with us, go not to Wittenberg.
HAMLET: I shall in all my best obey you Madam.
KING: Why 'tis a loving, and a fair reply,
Be as ourself in Denmark. Madam come,
This gentle and unforc'd accord of Hamlet
Sits smiling to my heart; in grace whereof,
No jocund health that Denmark drinks to-day,
But the great cannon to the clouds shall tell,
And the King's rouse, the heavens shall bruit again,
Re-speaking earthly thunder. Come away.

Flourish. Exeunt all but Hamlet.

HAMLET: Oh, that this too too solid flesh, would melt,
Thaw, and resolve itself into a dew:
Or that the Everlasting had not fix'd
His canon 'gainst self-slaughter. O God, O God!
How weary, stale, flat and unprofitable
Seems to me all the uses of this world!
Fie on't! oh fie, fie, 'tis an unweeded garden
That grows to seed: things rank, and gross in nature
Possess it merely. That it should come to this:
But two months dead: nay, not so much; not two,
So excellent a King, that was to this
Hyperion to a satyr: so loving to my mother,
That he might not beteem the winds of heaven
Visit her face too roughly. Heaven and earth
Must I remember: why she would hang on him,
As if increase of appetite had grown
By what it fed on; and yet within a month!
Let me not think on't: Frailty, thy name is woman.
A little month, or ere those shoes were old,
With which she followed my poor father's body
Like Niobe, all tears. Why she, even she,
(O Heaven! A beast that wants discourse of reason

Would have mourn'd longer) married with mine uncle,
My father's brother: but no more like my father,
Than I to Hercules. Within a month!
Ere yet the salt of most unrighteous tears
Had left the flushing of her galled eyes,
She married. O most wicked speed, to post
With such dexterity to incestuous sheets *:*
It is not, nor it cannot come to good.
But break my heart, for I must hold my tongue.

Enter Horatio, Bernardo, and Marcellus.

HORATIO: Hail to your Lordship.
HAMLET: I am glad to see you well:
Horatio, or I do forget myself.
HORATIO: The same my Lord, and your poor servant ever.
HAMLET: Sir my good friend, I'll change that name with you:
And what make you from Wittenberg Horatio?
Marcellus.
MARCELLUS: My good Lord.
HAMLET: I am very glad to see you: good even sir.
But what in faith make you from Wittenberg?
HORATIO: A truant disposition, good my Lord.
HAMLET: I would not have your enemy say so,
Nor shall you do mine ear that violence,
To make it truster of your own report
Against yourself. I know you are no truant:
But what is your affair in Elsinore?
We'll teach you to drink deep, ere you depart.
HORATIO: My Lord, I came to see your father's funeral.
HAMLET: I pray thee do not mock me, fellow-student.
I think it was to see my mother's wedding.
HORATIO: Indeed my Lord, it followed hard upon.
HAMLET: Thrift, thrift, Horatio: the funeral baked-meats
Did coldly furnish forth the marriage tables;
Would I had met my dearest foe in heaven,

Or I had ever seen that day Horatio.
My father, methinks I see my father.
HORATIO: Oh where my Lord?
HAMLET: In my mind's eye, Horatio.
HORATIO: I saw him once; he was a goodly King.
HAMLET: He was a man, take him for all in all :
I shall not look upon his like again.
HORATIO: My Lord, I think I saw him yesternight.
HAMLET: Saw? who?
HORATIO: My Lord, the King your father.
HAMLET: The King my father?
HORATIO: Season your admiration for a while
With an attent ear; till I may deliver
Upon the witness of these gentlemen,
This marvel to you.
HAMLET: For God's love let me hear.
HORATIO: Two nights together, had these gentlemen
(Marcellus and Bernardo) on their watch
In the dead waste and middle of the night
Been thus encounter'd. A figure like your father,
Arm'd at all points exactly, cap-a-pe,
Appears before them, and with solemn march
Goes slow and stately: by them thrice he walk'd,
By their oppress'd and fear-surprised eyes,
Within his truncheon's length; whilst they, distill'd
Almost to jelly with the act of fear,
Stand dumb and speak not to him. This to me
In dreadful secrecy impart they did,
And I with them the third night kept the watch,
Whereas they had deliver'd both in time,
Form of the thing, each word made true and good,
The apparition comes. I knew your father:
These hands are not more like.
HAMLET: But where was this?

MARCELLUS: My Lord upon the platform where we watch'd.
HAMLET: Did you not speak to it?
HORATIO: My Lord, I did;
But answer made it none: yet once methought
It lifted up its head, and did address
Itself to motion, like as it would speak:
But even then, the morning cock crew loud;
And at the sound it shrunk in haste away,
And vanish'd from our sight.
HAMLET: 'Tis very strange.
HORATIO: As I do live my honour'd Lord 'tis true;
And we did think it writ down in our duty
To let you know of it.
HAMLET: Indeed, indeed sirs; but this troubles me.
Hold you the watch to-night?
BOTH: We do my Lord.
HAMLET: Arm'd, say you?
BOTH; Arm'd, my Lord.
HAMLET: From top to toe?
BOTH: My Lord, from head to foot.
HAMLET: Then saw you not his face?
HORATIO: O yes, my Lord, he wore his beaver up.
HAMLET: What, look'd he frowningly?
HORATIO: A countenance more in sorrow than in anger.
HAMLET: Pale, or red?
HORATIO: Nay, very pale.
HAMLET: And fix'd his eyes upon you?
HORATIO: Most constantly.
HAMLET: I would I had been there.
HORATIO: It would have much amaz'd you.
HAMLET: Very like, very like: stay'd it long?
HORATIO: While one with moderate haste might tell a hundred.
BOTH: Longer, longer.
HORATIO: Not when I saw't.
HAMLET: His beard was grizzled, no?

HORATIO: It was, as I have seen it in his life,
A sable silver'd.
HAMLET: I will watch to-night;
Perchance 'twill walk again.
HORATIO: I warrant you it will.
HAMLET: If it assume my noble father's person,
I'll speak to it, though Hell itself should gape
And bid me hold my peace. I pray you all,
If you have hitherto conceal'd this sight;
Let it be tenable in your silence still:
And whatsoever else shall hap to-night,
Give it an understanding but no tongue;
I will requite your loves; so, fare you well:
Upon the platform 'twixt eleven and twelve,
I'll visit you.
ALL: Our duty to your Honour.

Exeunt.

HAMLET: Your love, as mine to you: farewell.
My father's spirit in arms? all is not well:
I doubt some foul play; would the night were come;
Till then sit still my soul; foul deeds will rise,
Though all the earth o'erwhelm them to men's eyes.

Exit.

I.3

Enter Laertes and Ophelia.

LAERTES: My necessaries are embark'd; farewell:
And sister, as the winds give benefit,
And convoy is assistant, do not sleep,
But let me hear from you.

OPHELIA: Do you doubt that?

LAERTES: For Hamlet, and the trifling of his favours,
Hold it a fashion and a toy in blood:
A violet in the youth of primy nature;
Froward, not permanent; sweet not lasting,
The perfume and suppliance of a minute,
No more.

OPHELIA: No more but so?

LAERTES: Think it no more:
For nature crescent does not grow alone,
In thews and bulk: but as this temple waxes,
The inward service of the mind and soul
Grows wide withal. Perhaps he loves you now,
And now no soil nor cautel doth besmirch
The virtue of his will: but you must fear,
His greatness weigh'd, his will is not his own;
For he himself is subject to his birth:
He may not, as unvalued persons do,
Carve for himself; for, on his choice depends
The sanctity and health of this whole State,
And therefore must his choice be circumscrib'd
Unto the voice and yielding of that body,
Whereof he is the head. Then if he says he loves you,
It fits your wisdom so far to believe it,
As he in his particular act and place
May give his saying deed: which is no further,
Than the main voice of Denmark goes withal.
Then weigh what loss your honour may sustain,
If with too credent ear you list his songs;
Or lose your heart; or your chaste treasure open
To his unmaster'd importunity.
Fear it Ophelia, fear it my dear sister,
And keep within the rear of your affection,
Out of the shot and danger of desire.
The chariest maid is prodigal enough,

If she unmask her beauty to the Moon:
Virtue itself 'scapes not calumnious strokes,
The canker galls the infants of the spring
Too oft before their buttons be disclos'd,
And in the morn and liquid dew of youth,
Contagious blastments are most imminent.
Be wary then, best safety lies in fear;
Youth to itself rebels, though none else near.

OPHELIA: I shall th' effect of this good lesson keep,
As watchman to my heart: but good my brother,
Do not as some ungracious pastors do,
Show me the steep and thorny way to heaven,
Whiles like a puff'd and reckless libertine
Himself, the primrose path of dalliance treads,
And wreaks not his own rede.

LAERTES: Oh, fear me not.

Enter Polonius.

I stay too long; but here my father comes:
A double blessing is a double grace;
Occasion smiles upon a second leave.

POLONIUS: Yet here Laertes? Aboard, aboard for shame,
The wind sits in the shoulder of your sail,
And you are stay'd for; there, my blessing with thee;
And these few precepts in thy memory,
See thou character. Give thy thoughts no tongue,
Nor any unproportion'd thought his act:
Be thou familiar; but by no means vulgar:
The friends thou hast, and their adoption tried,
Grapple them to thy soul, with hoops of steel:
But do not dull thy palm, with entertainment
Of each unhatch'd, unfledg'd, comrade. Beware
Of entrance to a quarrel: but being in
Bear't that th' opposed may beware of thee.
Give every man thine ear; but few thy voice:
Take each man's censure; but reserve thy judgment:

Costly thy habit as thy purse can buy;
But not express'd in fancy; rich, not gaudy:
For the apparel oft proclaims the man,
And they in France of the best rank and station,
Or of a most select and generous, chief in that.
Neither a borrower, nor a lender be;
For loan oft loses both itself and friend:
And borrowing dulls the edge of husbandry.
This above all; to thine ownself be true:
And it must follow, as the night the day,
Thou canst not then be false to any man.
Farewell: my blessing season this in thee.

LAERTES: Most humbly do I take my leave, my Lord.

POLONIUS: The time invites you, go, your servants tend.

LAERTES: Farewell Ophelia, and remember well
What I have said to you.

OPHELIA: 'Tis in my memory lock'd,
And you yourself shall keep the key of it.

LAERTES: Farewell.

Exit Laertes.

POLONIUS: What is't Ophelia he hath said to you?

OPHELIA: So please you, something touching the Lord Hamlet.

POLONIUS: Marry, well bethought:
'Tis told me he hath very oft of late
Given private time to you: and you yourself
Have of your audience been most free and bounteous.
If it be so, as so 'tis put on me;
And that in way of caution: I must tell you,
You do not understand yourself so clearly,
As it behoves my daughter, and your honour.
What is between you, give me up the truth.

OPHELIA: He hath my Lord of late, made many tenders
Of his affection for me.

POLONIUS: Affection, pooh. You speak like a green girl,

Unsifted in such perilous circumstance.
Do you believe his tenders, as you call them?
OPHELIA: I do not know, my Lord, what I should think.
POLONIUS: Marry I'll teach you; think yourself a baby,
That you have ta'en his tenders for true pay,
Which are not sterling. Tender yourself more dearly;
Or not to crack the wind of the poor phrase,
Roaming it thus, you'll tender me a fool.
OPHELIA: My Lord, he hath importun'd me with love,
In honourable fashion.
POLONIUS: Ay, fashion you may call it, go to, go to.
OPHELIA: And hath given countenance to his speech, my Lord,
With all the vows of Heaven.
POLONIUS: Ay, springes to catch woodcocks. I do know
When the blood burns, how prodigal the soul
Lends the tongue vows: these blazes, daughter,
Giving more light than heat, extinct in both,
Even in their promise, as it is a-making,
You must not take for fire. From this time
Be something scanter of your maiden presence;
Set your entreatments at a higher rate,
Than a command to parley. For Lord Hamlet,
Believe so much in him, that he is young,
And with a larger tether may he walk,
Than may be given you. In few, Ophelia,
Do not believe his vows; for they are brokers,
Not of that dye which their investments show,
But mere implorators of unholy suits,
Breathing like sanctified and pious bawds,
The better to beguile. This is for all :
I would not, in plain terms, from this time forth,
Have you so slander any moment leisure,
As to give words or talk with the Lord Hamlet:
Look to't, I charge you; come your ways.
OPHELIA: I shall obey my Lord.

Exeunt.

I.4

Enter Hamlet, Horatio, and Marcellus.

HAMLET: The air bites shrewdly: it is very cold.
HORATIO: It is a nipping and an eager air.
HAMLET: What hour now?
HORATIO: I think it lacks of twelve.
MARCELLUS: No, it is struck.
HORATIO: Indeed I heard it not: then it draws near the season,
Wherein the spirit held his wont to walk.
A flourish of trumpets, and two pieces go off.
What does this mean my Lord?
HAMLET: The King doth wake to-night, and takes his rouse,
Keeps wassail, and the swaggering up-spring reels:
And as he drains his draughts of Rhenish down,
The kettle-drum and trumpet thus bray out
The triumph of his pledge.
HORATIO: Is it a custom?
HAMLET: Ay marry is't;
But to my mind, though I am native here,
And to the manner born, it is a custom
More honour'd in the breach, than the observance.
[This heavy-headed revel east and west
Makes us traduc'd, and tax'd of other nations:
They clepe us drunkards, and with swinish phrase
Soil our addition; and indeed it takes
From our achievements, though perform'd at height,
The pith and marrow of our attribute:
So oft it chances in particular men,
That for some vicious mole of nature in them,
As in their birth wherein they are not guilty,
(Since nature cannot choose his origin)
By their o'ergrowth of some complexion

Oft breaking down the pales and forts of reason,
Or by some habit, that too much o'er-leavens
The form of plausive manners, that these men,
Carrying I say the stamp of one defect,
Being nature's livery, or fortune's star,
Their virtues else be they as pure as grace,
As infinite as man may undergo,
Shall in the general censure take corruption
From that particular fault: the dram of eale
Doth all the noble substance of a doubt
To his own scandal.]

Enter Ghost.

HORATIO: Look my Lord, it comes.
HAMLET: Angels and ministers of grace defend us:
Be thou a spirit of health, or goblin damn'd,
Bring with thee airs from Heaven, or blasts from Hell,
Be thy intents wicked or charitable,
Thou com'st in such a questionable shape
That I will speak to thee. I'll call thee Hamlet,
King, father, royal Dane: Oh, answer me,
Let me not burst in ignorance; but tell
Why thy canoniz'd bones hearsed in death,
Have burst their cerements, why the sepulchre
Wherein we saw thee quietly inurn'd,
Hath op'd his ponderous and marble jaws,
To cast thee up again? What may this meant?
That thou dead corse again in complete steel,
Revisit'st thus the glimpses of the Moon,
Making night hideous? and we fools of nature,
So horridly to shake our disposition,
With thoughts beyond the reaches of our souls;
Say, why is this? wherefore? what should we do?

Ghost beckons Hamlet.

HORATIO: It beckons you to go away with it,
As if it some impartment did desire
To you alone.
MARCELLUS: Look with what courteous action
It wafts you to a more removed ground:
But do not go with it.
HORATIO: No, by no means.
HAMLET: It will not speak: then I will follow it.
HORATIO: Do not my Lord.
HAMLET: Why, what should be the fear?
I do not set my life at a pin's fee;
And for my soul, what can it do to that,
Being a thing immortal as itself:
It waves me forth again; I'll follow it.
HORATIO: What if it tempt you toward the flood my Lord?
Or to the dreadful summit of the cliff,
That beetles o'er his base into the sea,
And there assume some other horrible form,
Which might deprive your sovereignty of reason,
And draw you into madness? think of it:
[The very place puts toys of desperation
Without more motive, into every brain
That looks so many fathoms to the sea
And hears it roar beneath.]
HAMLET: It wafts me still:
Go on, I'll follow thee.
MARCELLUS: You shall not go my Lord.
HAMLET: Hold off your hands.
HORATIO: Be rul'd, you shall not go.
HAMLET: My fate cries out,
And makes each petty arter in this body
As hardy as the Nemean lion's nerve:
Still am I call'd? Unhand me gentlemen:
By Heaven, I'll make a ghost of him that lets me:
I say away, go on, I'll follow thee.

Exeunt Ghost and Hamlet.

HORATIO: He waxes desperate with imagination.
MARCELLUS: Let's follow; 'tis not fit thus to obey him.
HORATIO: Have after, to what issue will this come?
MARCELLUS: Something is rotten in the state of Denmark.
HORATIO: Heaven will direct it.
MARCELLUS: Nay, let's follow him.

Exeunt.

I.5

Enter Ghost and Hamlet.

HAMLET: Where wilt thou lead me? speak; I'll go no further.
GHOST: Mark me.
HAMLET: I will.
GHOST: My hour is almost come,
When I to sulphurous and tormenting flames
Must render up myself.
HAMLET: Alas poor ghost.
GHOST: Pity me not, but lend thy serious hearing
To what I shall unfold.
HAMLET: Speak, I am bound to hear.
GHOST: So art thou to revenge, when thou shalt hear.
HAMLET: What?
GHOST: I am thy father's spirit,
Doom'd for a certain term to walk the night;
And for the day confin'd to fast in fires,
Till the foul crimes done in my days of nature
Are burnt and purg'd away. But that I am forbid
To tell the secrets of my prison-house,
I could a tale unfold, whose lightest word
Would harrow up thy soul, freeze thy young blood,

Make thy two eyes like stars, start from their spheres,
Thy knotty and combined locks to part,
And each particular hair to stand an end,
Like quills upon the fretful porpentine:
But this eternal blazon must not be
To ears of flesh and blood; list, Hamlet, oh list.
If thou didst ever thy dear father love.

HAMLET: O God!

GHOST: Revenge his foul and most unnatural murther.

HAMLET: Murther?

GHOST: Murther most foul, as in the best it is;
But this most foul, strange, and unnatural.

HAMLET: Haste, haste me to know it,
that I with wings as swift
As meditation, or the thoughts of love,
May sweep to my revenge.

GHOST: I find thee apt,
And duller shouldst thou be than the fat weed
That roots itself in ease on Lethe wharf,
Wouldn't thou not stir in this. Now Hamlet hear:
It's given out, that sleeping in my orchard,
A serpent stung me: so the whole ear of Denmark,
Is by a forged process of my death
Rankly abus'd: but know thou noble youth,
The serpent that did sting thy father's life,
Now wears his crown.

HAMLET: O my prophetic soul,
Mine uncle?

GHOST: Ay that incestuous, that adulterate beast
With witchcraft of his wits, with traitorous gifts
(O wicked wit, and gifts, that have the power
So to seduce!) won to his shameful lust
The will of my most seeming-virtuous Queen:
O Hamlet, what a falling-off was there,
From me, whose love was of that dignity,

That it went hand in hand, even with the vow
I made to her in marriage; and to decline
Upon a wretch whose natural gifts were poor
To those of mine.
But virtue, as it never will be moved,
Though lewdness court it in a shape of Heaven,
So lust, though to a radiant angel link'd,
Will sate itself in a celestial bed,
And prey on garbage.
But soft, methinks I scent the morning's air;
Brief let me be: sleeping within my orchard,
My custom always in the afternoon,
Upon my secure hour thy uncle stole
With juice of cursed hebonon in a vial,
And in the porches of mine ears did pour
The leperous distilment; whose effect
Holds such an enmity with blood of man,
That swift as quicksilver it courses through
The natural gates and alleys of the body;
And with a sudden vigour it doth posset
And curd, like eager droppings into milk,
The thin and wholesome blood: so did it mine;
And a most instant tetter bak'd about,
Most lazar-like, with vile and loathsome crust,
All my smooth body.
Thus was I, sleeping, by a brother's hand,
Of life, of crown, and Queen, at once dispatch'd;
Cut off even in the blossoms of my sin,
Unhousel'd, disappointed, unaneled.
No reckoning made, but sent to my account
With all my imperfections on my head;
O horrible, O horrible, most horrible;
If thou hast nature in thee bear it not;
Let not the royal bed of Denmark be
A couch for luxury and damned incest.

But howsoever thou pursuest this act,
Taint not thy mind; nor let thy soul contrive
Against thy mother aught; leave her to heaven,
And to those thorns that in her bosom lodge,
To prick and sting her. Fare thee well at once;
The glow-worm shows the matin to be near,
And 'gins to pale his uneffectual fire:
Adieu, adieu, Hamlet: remember me.

Exit.

HAMLET: Oh all you host of Heaven! Oh Earth: what else?
And shall I couple Hell? Oh fie: hold my heart;
And you my sinews grow not instant old;
But bear me stiffly up: remember thee?
Ay thou poor ghost, while memory holds a seat
In this distracted globe: remember thee?
Yea, from the table of my memory,
I'll wipe away all trivial fond records,
All saws of books, all forms, all pressures past,
That youth and observation copied there;
And thy commandment all alone shall live
Within the book and volume of my brain,
Unmix'd with baser matter; yes, yes, by Heaven:
O most pernicious woman!
Oh villain, villain, smiling damned villain!
My tables, my tables; meet it is I set it down,
That one may smile, and smile and be a villain;
At least I'm sure it may be so in Denmark;
So uncle there you are: now to my word;
It is; Adieu, adieu, remember me;
I have sworn't.

MARCELLUS: }
HORATIO: } *Within.* My Lord, my Lord.

Enter Horatio and Marcellus.

MARCELLUS: Lord Hamlet.
HORATIO: Heaven secure him.
HAMLET: So be it.
HORATIO: Illo, ho, ho, my Lord.
HAMLET: Hillo, ho, ho, boy; come bird, come.
MARCELLUS: How is't my noble Lord?
HORATIO: What news, my Lord?
HAMLET: O wonderful!
HORATIO: Good my Lord tell it.
HAMLET: No you will reveal it.
HORATIO: Not I, my Lord, by Heaven.
MARCELLUS: Nor I, my Lord.
HAMLET: How say you then, would heart of man once think it?
But you'll be secret?
BOTH: Ay, by Heaven, my Lord.
HAMLET: There's ne'er a villain dwelling in all Denmark
But he's an arrant knave.
HORATIO: There needs no ghost my Lord, come from the grave,
To tell us this.
HAMLET: Why right, you are i' th' right;
And so, without more circumstance at all,
I hold it fit that we shake hands, and part;
You, as your business and desire shall point you:
For every man hath business and desire,
Such as it is: and for my own part,
Look you, I'll go pray.
HORATIO: These are but wild and whirling words my Lord.
HAMLET: I'm sorry they offend you, heartily:
Yes faith, heartily.
HORATIO: There's no offence my Lord.
HAMLET: Yes, by Saint Patrick, but there is, Horatio,
And much offence too, touching this vision here:
It is an honest ghost, that let me tell you:
For your desire to know what is between us,
O'ermaster't as you may. And now good friends,

As you are friends, scholars and soldiers,
Give me one poor request.
HORATIO: What is't my Lord? we will.
HAMLET: Never make known what you have seen to-night.
BOTH: My Lord, we will not.
HAMLET: Nay, but swear't.
HORATIO: In faith my Lord, not I.
MARCELLUS; Nor I my Lord: in faith.
HAMLET: Upon my sword.
MARCELLUS: We have sworn my Lord already.
HAMLET: Indeed, upon my sword, indeed.

Ghost cries under the stage.

GHOST: Swear.
HAMLET: Ah ha boy say'st thou so? art thou there, truepenny?
Come on, you hear this fellow in the cellarage,
Consent to swear.
HORATIO: Propose the oath my Lord.
HAMLET: Never to speak of this that you have seen.
Swear by my sword.
GHOST: Swear.
HAMLET: *Hic et ubique?* Then we'll shift our ground.
Come hither gentlemen,
And lay your hands again upon my sword,
Never to speak of this that you have heard:
Swear by my sword.
GHOST: Swear.
HAMLET: Well said old mole, const work i' th' ground so fast?
A worthy pioner, once more remove good friends.
HORATIO: O day and night: but this is wondrous strange.
HAMLET: And therefore as a stranger give it welcome.
There are more things in Heaven and Earth, Horatio,
Than are dreamt of in our philosophy.
But come,

Here as before, never so help you mercy,
How strange or odd soe'er I bear myself;
As I perchance hereafter shall think meet
To put an antic disposition on:
That you at such times seeing me, never shall
With arms encumber'd thus, or thus, head-shake;
Or by pronouncing of some doubtful phrase;
As well, we know, or we could and if we would,
Or if we list to speak, or There be and if there might,
Or such ambiguous giving out to note,
That you know aught of me; this not to do:
So grace and mercy at your most need help you: Swear.

GHOST: Swear.

HAMLET: Rest, rest perturbed spirit: so gentlemen,
With all my love I do commend me to you;
And what so poor a man as Hamlet is,
May do t' express his love and friending to you,
God willing shall not lack: let us go in together,
And still your fingers on your lips I pray.
The time is out of joint: O cursed spite,
That ever I was born to set it right.
Nay, come let's go together.

Exeunt

II.I

Enter Polonius, and Reynaldo.

POLONIUS: Give him this money, and these notes Reynaldo.

REYNALDO: I will my Lord.

POLONIUS: You shall do marvellous wisely, good Reynaldo.

Before you visit him, to make inquire
Of his behaviour.
REYNALDO: My Lord, I did intend it.
POLONIUS: Marry, well said; very well said. Look you sir,
Inquire me first what Danskers are in Paris;
And how, and who: what means; and where they keep:
What company, at what expense: and finding
By this encompassment and drift of question,
That they do know my son, come you more nearer
Than your particular demands will touch it,
Take you as 'twere some distant knowledge of him,
As thus, I know his father and his friends,
And in part him. Do you mark this Reynaldo?
REYNALDO: Ay, very well my Lord.
POLONIUS: And in part him, but you may say, not well;
But if't be he I mean, he's very wild;
Addicted so and so; and there put on him
What forgeries you please: marry, none so rank,
As may dishonour him; take heed of that:
But sir, such wanton, wild, and usual slips,
As are companions noted and most known
To youth and liberty.
REYNALDO: As gaming my Lord.
POLONIUS: Ay, or drinking, fencing, swearing, quarrelling, drabbing.
You may go so far.
REYNALDO: My Lord that would dishonour him.
POLONIUS: Faith no, as you may season it in the charge;
You must not put another scandal on him,
That he is open to incontinency;
That's not my meaning: but breathe his faults so quaintly,
That they may seem the taints of liberty;
The flash and outbreak of a fiery mind,

A savageness in unreclaimed blood
Of general assault.

REYNALDO: But my good Lord–

POLONIUS: Wherefore should you do this?

REYNALDO: Ay my Lord,
I would know that.

POLONIUS: Marry sir, here's my drift,
And I believe it is a fetch of warrant:
You laying these slight sullies on my son,
As 'twere a thing a little soil'd i' th' working:
Mark you,
Your party in converse, him you would sound,
Having ever seen in the prenominate crimes,
The youth you breathe of guilty, be assur'd
He closes with you in this consequence:
Good sir, or so, or friend, or gentleman,
According to the phrase and the addition,
Of man and country.

REYNALDO: Very good my Lord.

POLONIUS: And then sir does he this, he does: what was I about to say? By the mass I was about to say something: where did I leave?

REYNALDO: At closes in the consequence: at friend, or so, and gentleman.

POLONIUS: At closes in the consequence, at marry,
He closes with you thus. I know the gentleman,
I saw him yesterday, or t'other day;
Or then, or then with such and such; and as you say,
There was a' gaming, there o'ertook in 's rouse,
There falling out at tennis; or perchance,
I saw him enter such a house of sale;
Videlicet, a brothel, or so forth.
See you now;

Your bait of falsehood, takes this carp of truth;
And thus do we of wisdom and of reach
With windlasses, and with assays of bias,
By indirections find directions out:
So by my former lecture and advice
Shall you my son; you have me, have you not?

REYNALDO: My Lord, I have.

POLONIUS: God buy you; fare you well.

REYNALDO; Good my Lord.

POLONIUS: Observe his inclination in yourself.

REYNALDO: I shall my Lord.

POLONIUS: And let him ply his music.

REYNALDO: Well, my Lord.

Exit

POLONIUS: Farewell:

Enter Ophelia.

How now Ophelia, what's the matter?

OPHELIA: Alas my Lord, I have been so affrighted.

POLONIUS: With what, in the name of Heaven?

OPHELIA: My Lord, as I was sewing in my chamber,
Lord Hamlet with his doublet all unbrac'd,
No hat upon his head, his stockings foul'd,
Ungarter'd, and down-gyved to his ankle,
Pale as his shirt, his knees knocking each other,
And with a look so piteous in purport,
As if he had been loosed out of hell,
To speak of horrors: he comes before me.

POLONIUS: Mad for thy love?

OPHELIA: My Lord, I do not know:
But truly I do fear it.

POLONIUS: What said he?

OPHELIA: He took me by the wrist, and held me hard;
Then goes he to the length of all his arm;
And with his other hand thus o'er his brow,
He falls to such perusal of my face
As he would draw it. Long stay'd he so;
At last, a little shaking of mine arm:
And thrice his head thus waving up and down;
He rais'd a sigh, so piteous and profound,
As it did seem to shatter all his bulk,
And end his being. That done, he lets me go,
And with his head over his shoulder turn'd,
He seem'd to find his way without his eyes,
For out a doors he went without their help;
And to the last bended their light on me.
POLONIUS: Come, go with me, I will go seek the King;
This is the very ecstasy of love,
Whose violent property fordoes itself,
And leads the will to desperate undertakings,
As oft as any passion under Heaven,
That does afflict our natures. I am sorry,
What, have you given him any hard words of late?
OPHELIA: No my good Lord: but as you did command,
I did repel his letters, and denied
His access to me.
POLONIUS: That hath made him mad.
I am sorry that with better heed and judgement
I had not quoted him. I fear'd he did but trifle,
And meant to wrack thee: but beshrew my jealousy:
It seems it is as proper to our age,
To cast beyond ourselves in our opinions,
As it is common for the younger sort
To lack discretion. Come, go we to the King,
This must be known, which being kept close might move
More grief to hide, than hate to utter love.
Come.

Exeunt.

II.2

Flourish.

Enter King and Queen, Rosencrantz and Guildenstern with others.

KING: Welcome dear Rosencrantz and Guildenstern.
Moreover, that we much did long to see you,
The need we have to use you, did provoke
Our hasty sending. Something have you heard
Of Hamlet's transformation: so I call it,
Sith nor th' exterior nor the inward man
Resembles that it was. What should it be
More than his father's death, that thus hath put him
So much from th' understanding of himself,
I cannot deem of: I entreat you both,
That being of so young days brought up with him:
And sith so neighbour'd to his youth, and humour,
That you vouchsafe your rest here in our Court
Some little time: so by your companies
To draw him on to pleasures, and to gather
So much as from occasions you may glean,
[Whether aught to us unknown afflicts him thus]
That open'd lies within our remedy.

QUEEN: Good gentlemen, he hath much talk'd of you,
And sure I am, two men there are not living,
To whom he more adheres. If it will please you
To show us so much gentry, and good will,
As to expend your time with us awhile,
For the supply and profit of our hope,
Your visitation shall receive such thanks
As fits a King's remembrance.

ROSENCRANTZ: Both your Majesties
Might by the sovereign power you have of us,
Put your dread pleasures, more into command
Than to entreaty.
GUILDENSTERN: We both obey,
And here give up ourselves, in the full bent,
To lay our services freely at your feet,
To be commanded.
KING: Thanks Rosencrantz, and gentle Guildenstern.
QUEEN: Thanks Guildernstern and gentle Rosencrantz.
And I beseech you instantly to visit
My too much changed son. Go some of ye,
And bring the gentlemen where Hamlet is.
GUILDENSTERN: Heavens make our presence and our practices
Pleasant and helpful to him.

Exeunt with others.

QUEEN: Ay, amen.

Enter Polonius.

POLONIUS: Th' ambassadors from Norway, my good Lord,
Are joyfully return'd.
KING: Thou still hast been the father of good news.
POLONIUS: Have I, my Lord? I assure you, my good Liege,
I hold my duty, as I hold my soul,
Both to my God, and to my gracious Kings:
And I do think, or else this brain of mine
Hunts not the trail of policy, so sure
As it hath used to do, that I have found
The very cause of Hamlet's lunacy.
KING: O speak of that, that do I long to hear.
POLONIUS: Give first admittance to th' ambassadors,
My news shall be the fruit to that great feast.
KING: Thyself do grace to them, and bring them in.

Exit Polonius.

He tells me my sweet Queen, that he hath found
The head and source of all your son's distemper.
QUEEN: I doubt it is no other, but the main,
His father death, and our o'erhasty marriage.

Enter Polonius, Voltemand and Cornelius

KING: Well, we shall sift him.
Welcome my good friends:
Say Voltemand, what from our brother Norway?
VOLTEMAND: Most fair return of greetings, and desires.
Upon our first, he sent us to suppress
His nephew's levies, which to him appear'd
To be a preparation 'gainst the Polack;
But better look'd into, he truly found
It was against your Highness, whereat grieved,
That so his sickness, age, and impotence
Was falsely borne in hand, sends out arrests
On Fortinbras, which he (in brief) obeys,
Receives rebuke from Norway: and in fine,
Makes vow before his uncle, never more
To give th' assay of arms against your Majesty.
Whereon old Norway, overcome with joy,
Gives him three thousand crowns in annual fee,
And his commission to employ those soldiers
So levied as before, against the Polack:
With an entreaty herein further shown,
That it might please you to give quiet pass
Through your dominions, for his enterprise,
On such regards of safety and allowance,
As therein are set down.
KING: It likes us well:
And at our more consider'd time we'll read,
Answer, and think upon this business.
Meantime we thank you, for your well-took labour.
Go to your rest, at night we'll feast together.
Most welcome home.

Exeunt Ambassadors.

POLONIUS: This business is very well ended.
My Liege, and Madam, to expostulate
What Majesty should be, what duty is,
Why day is day; night, night; and time is time,
Were nothing but to waste night, day, and time.
Therefore, since brevity is the soul of wit,
And tediousness, the limbs and outward flourishes,
I will be brief. Your noble son is mad:
Mad I call it; for to define true madness,
What is't, but to be nothing else but mad.
But let that go.

QUEEN: More matter, with less art.

POLONIUS: Madam, I swear I use no art at all :
That he is mad, 'tis true: 'tis true 'tis pity,
And pity it is true: a foolish figure,
But farewell it: for I will use no art.
Mad let us grant him then: and now remains
That we find out the cause of this effect,
Or rather say, the cause of this defect;
For this effect defective, comes by cause:
Thus it remains, and the remainder thus.
Perpend,
I have a daughter: have, while she is mine,
Who in her duty and obedience, mark,
Hath given me this: now gather, and surmise.

The Letter.

To the Celestial, and my Soul's idol, the most beautified Ophelia.

That's an ill phrase, a vile phrase, beautified is a vile phrase: but you shall hear:

These in her excellent white bosom, these &c.

QUEEN: Came this from Hamlet to her?

POLONIUS: Good Madam stay awhile, I will be faithful.

Doubt thou, the Stars are fire,
Doubt that the Sun doth move,
Doubt Truth to be a liar,
But never doubt, I love.

O dear Ophelia, I am ill at these numbers : I have not Art to reckon my groans; but that I love thee best, O most Best, believe it. Adieu.

Thine evermore most dear Lady,
whilst this machine is to him,
HAMLET.

This in obedience hath my daughter show'd me:
And more above hath his solicitings,
As they fell out by time, by means, and place,
All given to mine ear.

KING: But how hath she receiv'd his love?

POLONIUS: What do you think of me?

KING: As of a man, faithful and honourable.

POLONIUS: I would fain prove so. But what might you think?
When I had seen this hot love on the wing,
As I perceived it, I must tell you that
Before my daughter told me, what might you,
Or my dear Majesty your Queen here, think,
If I had play'd the desk or table-book,
Or given my heart a winking, mute and dumb,
Or look'd upon this love, with idle sight,
What might you think? No, I went round to work,
And my young mistress thus I did bespeak,
Lord Hamlet is a Prince out of thy star,
This must not be: and then, I precepts gave her,
That she should lock herself from his resort,
Admit no messengers, receive no tokens:
Which done, she took the fruits of my advice,
And he repulsed, a short tale to make,
Fell into a sadness, then into a fast,

Thence to a watch, thence into a weakness,
Thence to a lightness, and by this declension
Into the madness wherein now he raves,
And all we wail for.

KING: Do you think 'tis this?

QUEEN: It may be very likely.

POLONIUS: Hath there been such a time. I'ld fain know that,
That I have positively said, 'Tis so,
When it prov'd otherwise?

KING: Not that I know.

POLONIUS: Take this from this, if this be otherwise;
If circumstances lead me, I will find
Where truth is hid, though it were hid indeed
Within the Centre.

KING: How may we try it further?

POLONIUS: You know sometimes he walks four hours together,
Here in the lobby.

QUEEN: So he does indeed.

POLONIUS: At such a time I'll loose my daughter to him;
Be you and I behind an arras then;
Mark the encounter: if he love her not,
And be not from his reason fall'n thereon;
Let me be no assistant for a state,
But keep a farm and carters,

KING: We will try it.

Enter Hamlet, reading on a book.

QUEEN: But look where sadly the poor wretch comes reading.

POLONIUS: Away I do beseech you, both away,
I'll board him presently.

Exeunt King and Queen.

O give me leave.
How does my good Lord Hamlet?

HAMLET: Well, God-a-mercy.

POLONIUS: Do you know me, my Lord?

HAMLET: Excellent, excellent well: you are a fishmonger.

POLONIUS: Not I my Lord.

HAMLET: Then I would you were so honest a man.

POLONIUS: Honest, my Lord?

HAMLET: Ay sir, to be honest as this world goes, is to be one man pick'd out of two thousand.

POLONIUS: That's very true, my Lord.

HAMLET: For if the Sun breed maggots in a dead dog. being a good kissing carrion–Have you a daughter?

POLONIUS: I have my Lord.

HAMLET: Let her not walk i' th' Sun: conception is a blessing, but not as your daughter may conceive. Friend look to't.

POLONIUS: How say you by that? Still harping on my daughter yet he knew me not at first; he said I was a fishmonger: he is far gone, far gone, and truly in my youth, I suffered much extremity for love: very near this. I'll speak to him again. What do you read my Lord?

HAMLET: Words, words, words.

POLONIUS: What is the matter, my Lord?

HAMLET: Between who?

POLONIUS: I mean the matter that you read, my Lord.

HAMLET: Slanders sir: for the satirical slave says here, that old men have grey beards; that their faces are wrinkled; their eyes purging thick amber, or plum-tree gum: and that they have a plentiful lack of wit, together with weak hams. All which sir, though I most powerfully, and potently believe; yet I hold it not honesty to have it thus set down: for yourself sir, should be old as I am, if like a crab you could go backward.

POLONIUS: Though this be madness, yet there is method in't: will you walk out of the air my Lord?

HAMLET: Into my grave?

POLONIUS: Indeed that is out o' th 'air: how pregnant (sometimes) his replies are! a happiness, that often madness hits on, which reason and sanity could not so prosperously be deliver'd of. I will leave him, and suddenly contrive the means of meeting between him, and my daughter. My honourable Lord, I will most humbly take my leave of you.

HAMLET: You cannot sir take from me any thing, that I will more willingly part withal, except my life, my life.

POLONIUS: Fare you well my Lord.

HAMLET: These tedious old fools.

Enter Rosencrantz and Guildenstern.

POLONIUS: You go to seek my Lord Hamlet; there he is.

ROSENCRANTZ: God save you sir.

Exit Polonius.

GUILDENSTERN: My honour'd Lord!

ROSENCRANTZ: My most dear Lord!

HAMLET: My excellent good friends! How dost thou Guildenstern? Ah Rosencrantz; good lads: how do ye both?

ROSENCRANTZ: As the indifferent children of the earth.

GUILDENSTERN: Happy, in that we are not over-happy:
On Fortune's cap, we are not the very button.

HAMLET: Nor the soles of her shoe?

ROSENCRANTZ: Neither my Lord.

HAMLET: Then you live about her waist, or in the middle of her favour?

GUILDENSTERN: Faith, her privates, we.

HAMLET: In the secret parts of Fortune? Oh, most true: she is a strumpet. What's the news?

ROSENCRANTZ: None my Lord; but that the world's grown honest.

HAMLET: Then is Doomsday near: but your news is not true. Let me question more in particular: what have you my good friends, deserved at the hands of Fortune, that she sends you to prison hither?

GUILDENSTERN: Prison, my Lord?

HAMLET: Denmark's a prison.

ROSENCRANTZ: Then is the world one.

HAMLET: A goodly one, in which there are many confines, wards, and dungeons; Denmark being one o' th' worst.

ROSENCRANTZ: We think not so my Lord.

HAMLET: Why then 'tis none to you; for there is nothing either good or bad, but thinking makes it so: to me it is a prison.

ROSENCRANTZ: Why then your ambition makes it one: 'tis too narrow for your mind.

HAMLET: O God, I could be bounded in a nut-shell, and count myself a King of infinite space; were it not that I have bad dreams.

GUILDENSTERN: Which dreams indeed are ambition: for the very substance of the ambitious, is merely the shadow of a dream.

HAMLET: A dream itself is but a shadow.

ROSENCRANTZ: Truly, and I hold ambition of so airy and light a quality, that it is but a shadow's shadow.

HAMLET: Then are our beggars bodies, and our monarchs and outstretched heroes the beggars' shadows: shall we to th' Court: for, by my fay I cannot reason.

BOTH: We'll wait upon you.

HAMLET: No such matter. I will not sort you with the rest of my servants: for to speak to you like an honest man: I am most dreadfully attended: but in the beaten way of friendship, what make you at Elsinore?

ROSENCRANTZ: To visit you my Lord, no other occasion.

HAMLET: Beggar that I am, I am even poor in thanks; but I thank you: and sure dear friends my thanks are too dear a halfpenny; were you not sent for? Is it your own inclining? Is it a free visitation? Come, deal justly with me: come, come; nay speak.

GUILDENSTERN: What should we say my Lord?

HAMLET: Why any thing. But to the purpose; you were sent for; and there is a kind of confession in your looks ; which your modesties have not craft enough to colour, I know the good King and Queen have sent for you.

ROSENCRANTZ: To what end my Lord?

HAMLET: That you must teach me: but let me conjure you by the rights of our fellowship, by the consonancy of our youth, by the obligation of our ever-preserved love, and by what more dear, a better proposer could charge you withal; be even and direct with me, whether you were sent for or no.

ROSENCRANTZ: What say you?

HAMLET: Nay then I have an eye of you: if you love me hold not off.

GUILDENSTERN: My Lord, we were sent for.

HAMLET: I will tell you why; shall my anticipation prevent your discovery and your secrecy to the King and Queen, moult no feather: I have of late, but wherefore I know not, lost all my mirth, forgone all custom of exercise ; and indeed, it goes so heavily with my disposition; that this goodly frame the earth, seems to me a sterile promontory; this most excellent canopy the air, look you, this brave o'er-hanging firmament, this majestical roof, fretted with golden fire: why, it appears no other thing to me, than a foul and pestilent congregation of vapours. What a piece of work is a man! how noble in reason! how infinite in faculty! in form and moving how express and admirable! in action, how like an angel! in apprehension, how like a god! the beauty of the world, the paragon of animals; and yet to me, what is this quintessence of dust? man delights not me; no, nor woman neither; though by your smiling you seem to say so.

ROSENCRANTZ: My Lord, there was no such stuff in my thoughts.

HAMLET: Why did you laugh, when I said man delights not me?

ROSENCRANTZ: To think, my Lord, if you delight not in man, what lenten entertainment the Players shall receive from you: we coted them on the way, and hither are they coming to offer you service.

HAMLET: He that plays the King shall be welcome; his Majesty shall have tribute of me: the adventurous Knight shall use his foil and target: the lover shall not sigh *gratis*; the humorous man shall end his part in peace: the Clown shall make those laugh whose lungs are tickle o' th' sere: and the lady shall say her mind freely, or the blank verse shall halt for't: what Players are they?

ROSENCRANTZ: Even those you were wont to take delight in, the tragedians of the City.

HAMLET: How chances it they travel? their residence both in reputation and profit was better both ways.

ROSENCRANTZ: I think their inhibition comes by the means of the late innovation.

HAMLET: Do they hold the same estimation they did when I was in the City? are they so follow'd?

ROSENCRANTZ: No indeed, they are not.

HAMLET: How comes it? do they grow rusty?

ROSENCRANTZ: Nay, their endeavour keeps in the wonted pace; but there is sir an aery of children, little eyases, that cry out on the top of question; and are most tyrannically clapp'd for't: these are now the fashion, and so berattle the common Stages (so they call them) that many wearing rapiers, are afraid of goose-quills, and dare scarce come thither.

HAMLET: What, are they children? who maintains 'em? how are they escoted? Will they pursue the quality no longer than they can sing? will they not say afterwards if they should grow themselves to common Players (as it is most like if their means are no better) their writers do them wrong, to make them exclaim against their own succession?

ROSENCRANTZ: Faith there has been much to do on both sides: and the nation holds it no sin, to tarre them to controversy. There was for a while, no money bid for argument, unless the Poet and the Player went to cuffs in the question.

HAMLET: Is't possible?

GUILDENSTERN: O there has been much throwing about of brains.

HAMLET: Do the Boys carry it away?

ROSENCRANTZ: Ay that they do my Lord, Hercules and his load too.

HAMLET: It is not strange: for mine uncle is King of Denmark, and those that would make mows at him while my father lived, give twenty, forty, a hundred ducats a-piece for his picture in little. 'Sblood there is something in this more than natural, if Philosophy could find it out.

Flourish.

GUILDENSTERN: There are the Players.

HAMLET: Gentlemen, you are welcome to Elsinore: your hands, come: the appurtenance of welcome, is fashion and ceremony. Let me comply with you in the garb, lest my extent to the Players (which I tell you must show fairly outwards) should more appear like entertainment than yours. You are welcome: but my uncle-father, and aunt-mother are deceiv'd.

GUILDENSTERN: In what my dear Lord?

HAMLET: I am but mad north-north-west: when the wind is southerly, I know a hawk from a handsaw.

Enter Polonius.

POLONIUS: Well be with you gentlemen.

HAMLET: Hark you Guildenstern, and you too: at each ear a hearer: that great baby you see there, is not yet out of his swathing clouts.

ROSENCRANTZ: Happily he's die second time come to them: for they say, an old man is twice a child.

HAMLET: I will prophesy. He comes to tell me of the Players. Mark it. You say right sir: for a' Monday morning 'twas so indeed.

POLONIUS: My Lord, I have news to tell you.

HAMLET: My Lord, I have news to tell you. When Roscius was an actor in Rome —

POLONIUS: The actors are come hither my Lord.

HAMLET: Buz, buz.

POLONIUS: Upon my honour.

HAMLET: Then came each actor on his ass —

POLONIUS: The best actors in the world, either for Tragedy, Comedy, History, Pastoral, Pastoral-Comical, Historical-Pastoral: Tragical-Historical: Tragical-Comical-Historical-Pastoral: Scene individable, or Poem unlimited. Seneca cannot be too heavy, nor Plautus too light, for the law of writ, and the liberty. These are the only men.

HAMLET: O Jephthah Judge of Israel, what a treasure hadst thou?

POLONIUS: What a treasure had he, my Lord?

HAMLET: Why

One fair daughter, and no more,
The which he loved passing well.

POLONIUS: Still on my daughter.

HAMLET: Am I not i' th' right old Jephthah?

POLONIUS: If you call me Jephthah my Lord, I have a daughter that I love passing well.

HAMLET: Nay that follows not.

POLONIUS: What follows then, my Lord?

HAMLET: Why, as by lot, God wot: and then you know, it came to pass, as most like it was: the first row of the pious chanson will show you more. For look where my abridgements come.

Enter four or five Players.

You are welcome masters, welcome all. I am glad to see thee well: welcome good friends. O my old friend? thy face is valanced since I saw thee last: comest thou to beard me in Denmark? What, my young lady and mistress? By'r lady, your ladyship is nearer Heaven than when I saw you last, by the altitude of a chopine. Pray God your voice like a piece of uncurrent gold be not crack'd within the ring. Masters, you are welcome: we'll e'en to't like French falconers, fly at anything we see: we'll have a speech straight. Come give us a taste of your quality: come, a passionate speech.

FIRST PLAYER: What speech, my Lord?

HAMLET: I heard thee speak me a speech once, but it was never acted: or if it was, not above once, for the play I remembered pleas'd not the million, 'twas caviary to the general: but it was (as I receiv'd it, and others, whose judgements in such matters, cried in the top of mine) an excellent play; well digested in the scenes, set down with as much modesty, as cunning. I remember one said, there were no sallets in the lines, to make the matter savoury; nor no matter in the phrase, that might indict the author of affection, but call'd it an honest method. [As wholesome as sweet, and by very much more handsome than fine.] One chief speech in it I chiefly lov'd, 'twas Æneas' tale to Dido, and thereabout of it especially, where he speaks of Priam's slaughter. If it live in your memory, begin at this line, let me see, let me see:
'The rugged Pyrrhus like th' Hyrcanian beast.'
It is not so: it begins with Pyrrhus.
'The rugged Pyrrhus, he whose sable arms
Black as his purpose, did the night resemble
When he lay couched in the ominous horse,
Hath now this dread and black complexion smear'd
With heraldry more dismal: head to foot
Now is he total gules, horridly trick'd
With blood of fathers, mothers, daughters, sons,
Bak'd and impasted with the parching streets,
That lend a tyrannous, and damned light
To their vile murthers, roasted in wrath and fire,
And this o'er-sized with coagulate gore,
With eyes like carbuncles, the hellish Pyrrhus
Old grandsire Priam seeks.'

POLONIUS: 'Fore God, my Lord, well spoken, with good accent, and good discretion.

FIRST PLAYER: 'Anon he finds him,
Striking too short at Greeks. His antique sword,
Rebellious to his arm, lies where it falls
Repugnant to command: unequal match'd,
Pyrrhus at Priam drives, in rage strikes wide:
But with the whiff and wind of his fell sword,
Th' unnerved father falls. Then senseless Ilium,
Seeming to feel his blow, with flaming top
Stoops to his base, and with a hideous crash
Takes prisoner Pyrrhus' ear. For lo, his sword
Which was declining on the milky head
Of reverend Priam, seem'd i' th' air to stick:
So as a painted tyrant Pyrrhus stood,
And like a neutral to his will and matter,
Did nothing.
But as we often see against some storm,
A silence in the heavens, the rack stand still,
The bold winds speechless, and the orb below
As hush as death: anon the dreadful thunder
Doth rend the region. So after Pyrrhus' pause,
Aroused vengeance sets him new a-work,
And never did the Cyclops' hammers fall
On Mars his armours, forg'd for proof eterne,
With less remorse than Pyrrhus' bleeding sword
Now falls on Priam.
Out, out, thou strumpet Fortune, all you gods,
In general Synod take away her power:
Break all the spokes and fellies from her wheel,
And bowl the round nave down the hill of Heaven,
As low as to the fiends.'

POLONIUS: This is too long.

HAMLET: It shall to th' barber's, with your beard. Prithee say on: he's for a jig, or a tale of bawdry, or he sleeps. Say on; come to Hecuba.

FIRST PLAYER: 'But who, O who, had seen the mobled Queen.'

HAMLET: 'The mobled Queen?'

POLONIUS: That's good: 'mobled Queen' is good.

FIRST PLAYER: 'Run barefoot up and down, threatening the flame
With bisson rheum: a clout about that head
Where late the diadem stood, and for a robe
About her lank and all o'er-teemed loins,
A blanket in th' alarum of fear caught up.
Who this had seen, with tongue in venom steep'd,
'Gainst Fortune's state, would treason have pronounc'd;
But if the gods themselves did see her then,
When she saw Pyrrhus make malicious sport
In mincing with his sword her husband's limbs,
The instant burst of clamour that she made
(Unless things mortal move them not at all)
Would have made milch the burning eyes of Heaven,
And passion in the gods.'

POLONIUS: Look whe'er he has not turn'd his colour, and has tears in's eyes. Pray you no more.

HAMLET: 'Tis well, I'll have thee speak out the rest, soon. Good my Lord, will you see the Players well bestow'd. Do you hear, let them be well us'd for they are the abstracts and brief chronicles of the time. After your death, you were better have a bad epitaph, than their ill report while you live.

POLONIUS: My Lord, I will use them according to their desert.

HAMLET: God's bodykins man, better. Use every man after his desert, and who should 'scape whipping? Use them after your own honour and dignity. The less they deserve, the more merit is in your bounty. Take them in.

POLONIUS: Come sirs.

HAMLET: Follow him friends: we'll hear a play to-morrow *Exit Polonius and Players except the First Player.* Dost thou hear me old friend, can you play the Murther of Gonzago?

FIRST PLAYER: Ay my lord,

HAMLET: We'll ha't to-morrow night. You could for a need study a speech of some dozen or sixteen lines which I would set down, and insert in't? could you not?

FIRST PLAYER: Ay my Lord.

HAMLET: Very well. Follow that Lord, and look you mock him not. My good friends, I'll leave you till night, you are welcome to Elsinore.

ROSENCRANTZ: Good my Lord.

Exeunt.

Manet Hamlet.

HAMLET: Ay so, God buy ye: now I am alone.
Oh what a rogue and peasant slave am I!
Is it not monstrous that this Player here,
But in a fiction, in a dream of passion,
Could force his soul so to his whole conceit,
That from her working, all his visage wann'd;
Tears in his eyes, distraction in 's aspect,
A broken voice, and his whole function suiting
With forms, to his conceit? and all for nothing?
For Hecuba?
What's Hecuba to him, or he to Hecuba,
That he should weep for her? What would he do,
Had he the motive and the cue for passion
That I have? He would drown the stage with tears,
And cleave the general ear with horrid speech:
Make mad the guilty, and appal the free,
Confound the ignorant, and amaze indeed,
The very faculty of eyes and ears. Yet I,
A dull and muddy-mettled rascal, peak
Like John-a-dreams, unpregnant of my cause,
And can say nothing: no, not for a King,
Upon whose property, and most dear life,
A damn'd defeat was made. Am I a coward?
Who calls me villain? breaks my pate across?

Plucks off my beard, and blows it in my face?
Tweaks me by th' nose? gives me the lie i' th' throat,
As deep as to the lungs? who does me this?
Ha? Why, I should take it: for it cannot be,
But I am pigeon-liver'd, and lack gall
To make oppression bitter, or ere this,
I should have fatted all the region kites
With this slave's offal, bloody, bawdy villain,
Remorseless, treacherous, lecherous, kindless villain!
O Vengeance!
Why, what an ass am I? Ay sure, this is most brave,
That I, the son of the dear murthered,
Prompted to my revenge by Heaven, and Hell,
Must (like a whore) unpack my heart with words,
And fall a-cursing like a very drab.
A scullion! Fie upon't: foh. About my brain.
I have heard, that guilty creatures sitting at a play.
Have by the very cunning of the scene,
Been struck so to the soul, that presently
They have proclaim'd their malefactions,
For murther, though it have no tongue, will speak
With most miraculous organ. I'll have these Players,
Play something like the murder of my father,
Before mine uncle. I'll observe his looks,
I'll tent him to the quick: if he but blench
I know my course. The spirit that I have seen
May be the Devil, and the Devil hath power
T' assume a pleasing shape, yea and perhaps
Out of my weakness, and my melancholy,
As he is very potent with such spirits,
Abuses me to damn me. I'll have grounds
More relative than this: the play's the thing,
Wherein I'll catch the conscience of the King.

Exit.

III.I

Enter King, Queen, Polonius, Ophelia, Rosencrantz, Guildenstern, and Lords.

KING: And can you by no drift of circumstance
Get from him why he puts on this confusion,
Grating so harshly all his days of quiet
With turbulent and dangerous lunacy?
ROSENCRANTZ: He does confess he feels himself distracted, But from what cause he will by no means speak.
GUILDENSTERN: Nor do we find him forward to be sounded,
But with a crafty madness keeps aloof,
When we would bring him on to some confession of his true state.
QUEEN: Did he receive you well?
ROSENCRANTZ: Most like a gentleman.
GUILDENSTERN: But with much forcing of his disposition.
ROSENCRANTZ: Niggard of question, but of our demands most free in his reply.
QUEEN: Did you assay him to any pastime?
ROSENCRANTZ: Madam, it so fell out, that certain Players
We o'er-raught on the way: of these we told him,
And there did seem in him a kind of joy
To hear of it: they are about the Court,
And (as I think) they have already order
This night to play before him.
POLONIUS: 'Tis most true:
And he beseech'd me to entreat your Majesties
To hear, and see the matter.
KING: With all my heart, and it doth much content me
To hear him so inclin'd.
Good gentlemen, give him a further edge,
And drive his purpose on to these delights.

ROSENCRANTZ: We shall my Lord.

Exeunt Rosencrantz and Guildenstern.

KING: Sweet Gertrude leave us too,
For we have closely sent for Hamlet hither,
That he, as 'twere by accident, may here
Affront Ophelia.
Her father, and myself (lawful espials),
Will, so bestow ourselves, that seeing unseen
We may of their encounter frankly judge,
And gather by him, as he is behav'd,
If't be th' affliction of his love, or no,
That thus he suffers for.

QUEEN: I shall obey you,
And for your part Ophelia, I do wish
That your good beauties be the happy cause
Of Hamlet's wildness: so shall I hope your virtues
Will bring him to his wonted way again,
To both your honours.

OPHELIA: Madam, I wish it may.

Exit Queen.

POLONIUS: Ophelia, walk you here. Gracious so please you
We will bestow ourselves: read on this book,
That show of such an exercise may colour
Your loneliness. We are oft to blame in this,
'Tis too much prov'd, that with Devotion's visage,
And pious action, we do sugar o'er
The devil himself.

KING: O 'tis too true!
How smart a lash that speech doth give my conscience!
The harlot's cheek beautied with plastering art
Is not more ugly to the thing that helps it,
Than is my deed, to my most painted word.
O heavy burthen!

POLONIUS: I hear him coming, let's withdraw my Lord.

Exeunt.

Enter Hamlet.

HAMLET: To be, or not to be, that is the question:
Whether 'tis nobler in the mind to suffer
The slings and arrows of outrageous Fortune,
Or to take arms against a sea of troubles,
And by opposing end them: to die to sleep;
No more; and by a sleep, to say we end
The heart-ache, and the thousand natural shocks
That flesh is heir to? 'tis a consummation
Devoutly to be wish'd. To die to sleep,
To sleep, perchance to dream; ay, there's the rub,
For in that sleep of death, what dreams may come,
When we have shuffled off this mortal coil,
Must give us pause. There's the respect
That makes calamity of so long life:
For who would bear the whips and scorns of time,
The oppressor's wrong, the proud man's contumely,
The pangs of dispiz'd love, the Law's delay,
The insolence of office, and the spurns
That patient merit of the unworthy takes,
When he himself might his quietus make,
With a bare bodkin? who would fardels bear,
To grunt and sweat under a weary life,
But that the dread of something after death,
The undiscovered country, from whose bourn
No traveller returns, puzzles the will,
And makes us rather bear those ills we have,
Than fly to others that we know not of
Thus conscience does make cowards of us all,
And thus the native hue of resolution
Is sickbed o'er, with the pale cast of thought,
And enterprises of great pith and moment,

With this regard their currents turn awry,
And lose the name of action. Soft you now,
The fair Ophelia? Nymph, in thy orisons
Be all my sins remember'd.

OPHELIA: Good my Lord,
How does your honour for this many a day?

HAMLET: I humbly thank you: well, well, well.

OPHELIA: My Lord, I have remembrances of yours,
That I have longed long to re-deliver.
I pray you now, receive them.

HAMLET: No, no, I never gave you aught.

OPHELIA: My honour'd Lord, I know right well you did,
And with them words of so sweet breath compos'd,
As made the things more rich, their perfume left:
Take these again, for to the noble mind,
Rich gifts wax poor, when givers prove unkind.
There my Lord.

HAMLET: Ha, ha: are you honest?

OPHELIA: My Lord.

HAMLET: Are you fair?

OPHELIA: What means your Lordship?

HAMLET: That if you be honest and fair, your honesty should admit no discourse to your beauty.

OPHELIA: Could beauty my Lord, have better commerce than with honesty?

HAMLET: Ay, truly: for the power of beauty will sooner transform honesty from what it is, to a bawd, than the force of honesty can translate beauty into his likeness. This was sometime a paradox, but now the time gives it proof. I did love you once.

OPHELIA: Indeed my Lord, you made me believe so.

HAMLET: You should not have believed me. For virtue, cannot so inoculate our old stock, but we shall relish of it.
I loved you not.

OPHELIA: I was the more deceived.

HAMLET: Get thee to a nunnery. Why wouldst thou be a breeder of sinners? I am myself indifferent honest, but yet I could accuse me of such things, that it were better my mother had not borne me. I am very proud, revengeful, ambitious, with more offences at my beck, than I have thoughts to put them in, imagination to give them shape, or time to act them in. What should such fellows as I do, crawling between Heaven and earth. We are arrant knaves all, believe none of us. Go thy ways to a nunnery. Where's your father?

OPHELIA: At home, my Lord.

HAMLET: Let the doors be shut upon him, that he may play the fool no where but in's own house. Farewell.

OPHELIA: O help him, you sweet Heavens.

HAMLET: If thou dost marry, I'll give thee this plague for thy dowry. Be thou as chaste as ice, as pure as snow, thou shalt not escape calumny. Get thee to a nunnery. Go, farewell. Or, if thou wilt needs marry, marry a fool: for wise men know well enough, what monsters you make of them. To a nunnery go, and quickly too. Farewell.

OPHELIA: O heavenly powers, restore him.

HAMLET: I have heard of your paintings too well enough. God has given you one face, and you make yourselves another: you jig, you amble, and you lisp, and nickname God's creatures, and make your wantonness, your ignorance. Go to, I'll no more on't, it hath made me mad. I say, we will have no more marriages. Those that are married already, all but one shall live, the rest shall keep as they are. To a nunnery, go.

Exit Hamlet.

OPHELIA: O what a noble mind is here o'erthrown!
The courtier's, soldier's, scholar's eye, tongue, sword,
Th' expectancy and rose of the fair State,
The glass of fashion, and the mould of form,

Th' observ'd of all observers, quite, quite down.
And I of ladies most deject and wretched,
That suck'd the honey of his music vows;
Now see that noble, and most sovereign reason,
Like sweet bells jangled out of tune, and harsh,
That unmatch'd form and feature of blown youth,
Blasted with ecstasy. O woe is me,
T' have seen what I have seen: see what I see.

Enter King and Polonius.

KING: Love? his affections do not that way tend,
Nor what he spake, though it lack'd form a little,
Was not like madness. There's something in his soul,
O'er which his melancholy sits on brood,
And I do doubt the hatch, and the disclose
Will be some danger, which for to prevent
I have in quick determination
Thus set it down.
He shall with speed to England
For the demand of our neglected tribute:
Haply the seas and countries different
With variable objects, shall expel
This something-settled matter in his heart:
Whereon his brains still beating puts him thus
From fashion of himself. What think you on't?

POLONIUS: It shall do well. But yet do I believe
The origin and commencement of his grief
Sprung from neglected love. How now Ophelia:
You need not tell us, what Lord Hamlet said,
We heard it all. My Lord, do as you please,
But if you hold it fit after the play,
Let his Queen mother all alone entreat him
To show his grief: let her be round with him
And I'll be plac'd, so please you, in the ear
Of all their conference. If she find him not,

To England send him: or confine him where
Your wisdom best shall think.

KING: It shall be so:
Madness in great ones, must not unwatch'd go.

Exeunt.

III.2

Enter Hamlet, and two or three of the Players.

HAMLET: Speak the speech I pray you as I pronounc'd it to you trippingly on the tongue: but if you mouth it, as many of your Players do, I had as lief the town-crier had spoke my lines: nor do not saw the air too much with your hand thus, but use all gently; for in the very torrent, tempest, and (as I may say) the whirlwind of passion, you must acquire and beget a temperance that may give it smoothness. O it offends me to the soul, to hear a robustious periwig-pated fellow tear a passion to tatters, to very rags, to split the ears of the groundlings; who (for the most part) are capable of nothing, but inexplicable dumb-shows, and noise: I could have such a fellow whipped for o'erdoing Termagant: it out-herods Herod. Pray you avoid it.

PLAYER: I warrant your Honour.

HAMLET: Be not too tame neither: but let your own discretion be your tutor. Suit the action to the word, the word to the action, with this special observance: that you o'erstep not the modesty of Nature: for any thing so overdone, is from the purpose of playing, whose end both at the first and now, was and is, to hold as 'twere the mirror up to Nature; to show Virtue her own feature, Scorn her own image, and the very age and body of the time, his form and pressure. Now, this overdone, or come tardy off, though it make the unskilful laugh, cannot but make the judicious grieve; the censure of the which one, must in your allowance o'erweigh a whole theatre of others. Oh, there be Players that I have seen play, and heard others praise, and that highly (not to speak it profanely) that neither having the accent of Christians, nor the gait of Christian, pagan, nor man, have so strutted and bellowed, that I have thought some of Nature's journeymen had made men, and not made them well, they imitated humanity so abominably.

FIRST PLAYER: I hope we have reform'd that indifferently with us, sir.

HAMLET: O reform it altogether. And let those that play your Clowns, speak no more than is set down for them. For there be of them, that will themselves laugh, to set on some quantity of barren spectators to laugh too, though in the mean time, some necessary question of the play be then to be considered: that's villainous, and shows a most pitiful ambition in the Fool that uses it. Go make you ready.

Exeunt Players.

Enter Polonius, Rosencrantz, and Guildenstern.

How now my Lord, will the King hear this piece of work?

POLONIUS: And the Queen too, and that presently.

HAMLET: Bid the Players make haste.

Exit Polonius.

Will you two help to hasten them?

BOTH: We will my Lord.

Exeunt.

Enter Horatio.

HAMLET: What ho, Horatio?

HORATIO: Here sweet Lord, at your service.

HAMLET: Horatio, thou art e'en as just a man as e'er my conversation cop'd withal.

HORATIO: O my dear Lord.

HAMLET: Nay, do not think I flatter:
For what advancement may I hope from thee,
That no revenue hast, but thy good spirits
To feed and clothe thee? Why should the poor be flatter'd?
No, let the candied tongue, lick absurd pomp,
And crook the pregnant hinges of the knee,
Where thrift may follow fawning; dost thou hear,
Since my dear soul was mistress of my choice,
And could of men distinguish, her election
Hath seal'd thee for herself. For thou hast been
As one in suffering all, that suffers nothing.
A man that Fortune's buffets, and rewards
Hath ta'en with equal thanks. And blest are those,
Whose blood and judgement are so well commingled,
That they are not a pipe for Fortune's finger,
To sound what stop she please. Give me that man,
That is not passion's slave, and I will wear him
In my heart's core, ay, in my heart of heart,
As I do thee. Something too much of this.
There is a play to-night before the King;
One scene of it comes near the circumstance
Which I have told thee, of my father's death.
I prithee, when thou seest that act afoot,
Even with the very comment of thy soul
Observe mine uncle: if his occulted guilt,
Do not itself unkennel in one speech,
It is a damned ghost that we have seen:
And my imaginations are as foul
As Vulcan's stithy. Give him heedful note,
For I mine eyes will rivet to his face:
And after we will both our judgements join,
To censure of his seeming.

HORATIO: Well, my Lord.
If he steal aught the whilst this play is playing,
And 'scape detecting, I will pay the theft.

Enter trumpets and kettledrums.

HAMLET: They are coming to the play: I must be idle.
Get you a place.

Enter King, Queen, Polonius, Ophelia, Rosencrantz, Guildenstern, and other Lords attendant, with his Guard carrying torches. Danish March. Sound a flourish.

KING: How fares our Cousin Hamlet?

HAMLET: Excellent i' faith, of the chameleon's dish: I eat the air, promise-cramm'd, you cannot feed capons so.

KING: I have nothing with this answer Hamlet, these words are not mine.

HAMLET: No, nor mine. Now my Lord, you played once i' th' university, you say?

POLONIUS: That I did my Lord, and was accounted a good actor.

HAMLET: What did you enact?

POLONIUS: I did enact Julius Cæsar, I was kill'd i' th'
Capitol: Brutus kill'd me.

HAMLET: It was a brute part of him, to kill so capital a calf there. Be the Players ready?

ROSENCRANTZ: Ay my Lord, they stay upon your patience.

QUEEN: Come hither my good Hamlet, sit by me.

HAMLET: No, good mother, here's metal more attractive.

POLONIUS: O ho, do you mark that?

HAMLET: Lady, shall I lie in your lap?

OPHELIA: No, my Lord.

HAMLET: I mean, my head upon your lap?

OPHELIA: Ay, my Lord.

HAMLET: Do you think I meant country matters?

OPHELIA: I think nothing, my Lord.

HAMLET: That's a fair thought to lie between maids' legs.

OPHELIA: What is, my Lord?

HAMLET: Nothing.

OPHELIA: You are merry, my Lord?

HAMLET: Who I?

OPHELIA: Ay, my Lord.

HAMLET: O God, your only jig-maker: what should a man do, but be merry? for look you how cheerfully my mother looks, and my father died within's two hours.

OPHELIA: Nay, 'tis twice two months, my Lord.

HAMLET: So long? Nay then let the Devil wear black, for I'll have a suit of sables. O Heavens! die two months ago, and not forgotten yet? Then there's hope, a great man's memory, may outlive his life half a year: but by'r lady he must build churches then: or else shall he suffer not thinking on, with the hobby-horse, whose epitaph is, 'For O, for O, the hobby-horse is forgot.'

Hautboys play. The dumb-show enters.

Enter a King and Queen, very lovingly; the Queen embracing him and he her. She kneels and makes show of protestation unto him. He takes her up, and declines his head upon her neck; lays him down upon a bank of flowers. She seeing him asleep, leaves him. Anon comes in a fellow, takes off his crown, kisses it, and pours poison in the King's ears, and exits. The Queen returns, finds the King dead, and makes passionate action. The Poisoner, with some two or three Mutes comes in again, seeming to lament with her. The dead body is carried away: the Poisoner wooes the Queen with gifts, she seems loath and unwilling awhile, but in the end accepts his love.

Exeunt.

OPHELIA: What means this, my Lord?

HAMLET: Marry this is miching mallecho, that means mischief.

OPHELIA: Belike this show imports the argument of the play.

HAMLET: We shall know by these fellows: the Players cannot keep counsel: they'll tell all.

OPHELIA: Will he tell us what this show meant?

HAMLET: Ay, or any show that you will show him. Be not you ashamed to show, he'll not shame to tell you what it means.

OPHELIA: You are naught, you are naught, I'll mark the play.

Enter Prologue.

PROLOGUE: For us, and for our tragedy,
Here stooping to your clemency:
We beg your hearing patiently.

Exit.

HAMLET: Is this a prologue, or the posy of a ring?

OPHELIA: 'Tis brief, my Lord.

HAMLET: As woman's love.

Enter two Players, King and his Queen.

PLAYER KING: Full thirty times hath Phœbus' cart gone round,
Neptune's salt wash, and Tellus' orbed ground:
And thirty dozen Moons with borrow'd sheen,
About the world have times twelve thirties been,
Since love our hearts, and Hymen did our hands
Unite commutual, in most sacred bands.

PLAYER QUEEN: So many journeys may the Sun and Moon
Make us again count o'er, ere love be done.
But woe is me, you are so sick of late,
So far from cheer, and from your former state
That I distrust you: yet though I distrust,
Discomfort you, my Lord, it nothing must:
For women's fear and love, holds quantity,
In neither aught, or in extremity:
Now what my love is, proof hath made you know,
And as my love is siz'd, my fear is so:
[Where love is great, the littlest doubts are fear,
Where little fears grow great, great love grows there.]

PLAYER KING: Faith I must leave thee love, and shortly too:
My operant powers their functions leave to do:
And thou shalt live in this fair world behind,

Honour'd, belov'd, and haply, one as kind
For husband shalt thou —

PLAYER QUEEN: O confound the rest:
Such love, must needs be treason in my breast:
In second husband let me be accurst,
None wed the second, but who kill'd the first.

HAMLET: Wormwood, wormwood.

PLAYER QUEEN: The instances that second marriage move,
Are base respects of thrift, but none of love.
A second time, I kill my husband dead,
When second husband kisses me in bed,

PLAYER KING: I do believe you think what now you speak:
But what we do determine, oft we break:
Purpose is but the slave to memory,
Of violent birth, but poor validity:
Which now like fruit unripe sticks on the tree,
But fall unshaken, when they mellow be.
Most necessary 'tis, that we forget
To pay ourselves, what to ourselves is debt:
What to ourselves in passion we propose,
The passion ending, doth the purpose lose.
The violence of either grief or joy,
Their own enactures with themselves destroy:
Where joy most revels, grief doth most lament;
Grief joys, joy grieves on slender accident.
This world is not for aye, nor 'tis not strange
That even our loves should with our fortunes change.
For 'tis a question left us yet to prove,
Whether Love lead Fortune, or else Fortune Love.
The great man down, you mark his favourite flies,
The poor advanc'd, makes friends of enemies:
And hitherto doth Love on Fortune tend,
For who not needs, shall never lack a friend:
And who in want a hollow friend doth try,

Directly seasons him his enemy.
But orderly to end, where I begun,
Our wills and fates do so contrary run,
That our devices still are overthrown,
Our thoughts are ours, their ends none of our own.
So think thou wilt no second husband wed:
But die thy thoughts, when thy first Lord is dead.

PLAYER QUEEN: Nor earth to me give food, nor Heaven light,
Sport and repose lock from me day and night:
[To desperation turn my trust and hope,
An anchor's cheer in prison be my scope:]
Each opposite that blanks the face of joy,
Meet what I would have well, and it destroy:
Both here, and hence, pursue me lasting strife,
If once a widow, ever I be wife.

HAMLET: If she should break it now.

PLAYER KING: 'Tis deeply sworn: sweet, leave me here awhile,
My spirits grow dull, and fain I would beguile
The tedious day with sleep.

Sleeps.

PLAYER QUEEN: Sleep rock thy brain,
And never come mischance between us twain.

Exit.

HAMLET: Madam, how like you this play?

QUEEN: The lady protests too much methinks.

HAMLET: O but she'll keep her word.

KING: Have you heard the argument? Is there no offence in't?

HAMLET: No, no, they do but jest, poison in jest, no offence i' th' world.

KING: What do you call the play?

HAMLET: The Mouse-trap: marry how? Tropically: this play is the image of a murder done in Vienna: Gonzago is the Duke's name, his wife Baptista: you shall see anon: 'tis a knavish piece of work: but what o' that? your Majesty, and we that have free souls, it touches us not: let the gall'd jade winch, our withers are unwrung.

Enter Lucianus.

This is one Lucianus nephew to the King.

OPHELIA: You are a good Chorus, my Lord.

HAMLET: I could interpret between you and your love: if I could see the puppets dallying.

OPHELIA: You are keen my Lord, you are keen.

HAMLET: It would cost you a groaning, to take off my edge.

OPHELIA: Still better and worse.

HAMLET: So you must take husbands. Begin murderer. Pox, leave thy damnable faces, and begin. Come, the croaking raven doth bellow for revenge.

LUCIANUS: Thoughts black, hands apt, drugs fit, and time agreeing:
Confederate season, else, no creature seeing:
Thou mixture rank, of midnight weeds collected,
With Hecat's ban, thrice blasted, thrice infected,
Thy natural magic, and dire property,
On wholesome life, usurp immediately.

Pours the poison in his ears.

HAMLET: He poisons him i' th' garden for 's estate: his name's Gonzago: the story is extant and writ in choice Italian. You shall see anon how the murtherer gets the love of Gonzago's wife.

OPHELIA: The King rises.

HAMLET: What, frighted with false fire?

QUEEN: How fares my Lord?

POLONIUS: Give o'er the play.

KING: Give me some light. Away.

ALL: Lights, lights, lights.

Exeunt all but Hamlet and Horatio.

HAMLET: Why let the stricken deer go weep,
  The hart ungalled play:
For some must watch, while some must sleep;
  So runs the world away.
Would not this sir, and a forest of feathers, if the rest of my fortunes turn Turk with me, with two Provincial roses on my raz'd shoes, get me a fellowship in a cry of Players, sir?

HORATIO: Half a share.

HAMLET: A whole one I,
For thou dost know: O Damon dear,
This realm dismantled was
Of Jove himself, and now reigns here
A very very pajock.

HORATIO: You might have rhymed.

HAMLET: Oh good Horatio, I'll take the Ghost's word for a thousand pound. Didst perceive?

HORATIO: Very well my Lord.

HAMLET: Upon the talk of the poisoning?

HORATIO: I did very well note him.

Enter Rosencrantz and Guildenstern.

HAMLET: Oh, ha? Come some music. Come the recorders :
For if the King like not the comedy,
Why then belike he likes it not perdy.
Come some music.

GUILDENSTERN: Good my Lord, vouchsafe me a word with you.

HAMLET: Sir, a whole history.

GUILDENSTERN: The King, sir.

HAMLET: Ay sir, what of him?

GUILDENSTERN: Is in his retirement, marvellous distemper'd.

HAMLET: With drink sir?

GUILDENSTERN: No my Lord, rather with choler.

HAMLET: Your wisdom should show itself more richer, to signify this to his doctor: for, for me to put him to his purgation, would perhaps plunge him into far more choler.

GUILDENSTERN: Good my Lord put your discourse into some frame, and start not so wildly from my affair.

HAMLET: I am tame sir, pronounce.

GUILDENSTERN: The Queen your mother, in most great affliction of spirit, hath sent me to you.

HAMLET: You are welcome.

GUILDENSTERN: Nay, good my Lord, this courtesy is not of the right breed. If it shall please you to make me a wholesome answer, I will do your mother's commandment: if not, your pardon, and my return shall be the end of my business.

HAMLET: Sir, I cannot.

GUILDENSTERN: What, my Lord?

HAMLET: Make you a wholesome answer: my wit's diseased. But, sir, such answer as I can make, you shall command: or rather as you say, my mother: therefore no more but to the matter. My mother you say —

ROSENCRANTZ: Then thus she says: your behaviour hath struck her into amazement, and admiration.

HAMLET: O wonderful son, that can so astonish a mother. But is there no sequel at the heels of this mother's admiration?

ROSENCRANTZ: She desires to speak with you in her closet, ere you go to bed.

HAMLET: We shall obey, were she ten times our mother.
Have you any further trade with us?

ROSENCRANTZ: My Lord, you once did love me.

HAMLET: So I do still, by these pickers and stealers.

ROSENCRANTZ: Good my Lord, what is your cause of distemper? you do surely bar the door of your own liberty, if you deny your griefs to your friend.

HAMLET: Sir I lack advancement.

ROSENCRANTZ: How can that be, when you have the voice of the king himself, for your succession in Denmark?

HAMLET: Ay, but while the grass grows, the proverb is something musty.

Enter one with a recorder.

O the recorder. Let me see, to withdraw with you, why do you go about to recover the wind of me, as if you would drive me into a toil?

GUILDENSTERN: O my Lord, if my duty be too bold, my love is too unmannerly.

HAMLET: I do not well understand that. Will you play upon this pipe?

GUILDENSTERN: My Lord, I cannot.

HAMLET: I pray you.

GUILDENSTERN: Believe me, I cannot.

HAMLET: I do beseech you.

GUILDENSTERN: I know no touch of it, my Lord.

HAMLET: 'Tis as easy as lying: govern these ventages with your finger and thumb, give it breath with your mouth, and it will discourse most eloquent music. Look you, these are the stops.

GUILDENSTERN: But these cannot I command to any utterance of harmony, I have not the skill.

HAMLET: Why look you now, how unworthy a thing you make of me: you would play upon me; you would seem to know my stops: you would pluck out the heart of my mystery; you would sound me from my lowest note, to the top of my compass: and there is much music, excellent voice, in this little organ, yet cannot you make it speak. Why do you think that I am easier to be played on, than a pipe? Call me what instrument you will, though you can fret me, you cannot play upon me.
God bless you sir.

Enter Polonius.

POLONIUS: My Lord; the Queen would speak with you, and presently.

HAMLET: Do you see that cloud? that's almost in shape like a camel.

POLONIUS: By th' mass, and it's like a camel indeed.

HAMLET: Methinks it is like a weazel.
POLONIUS: It is back'd like a weazel.
HAMLET: Or like a whale?
POLONIUS: Very like a whale.
HAMLET: Then I will come to my mother, by and by; They fool me to the top of my bent. I will come by and by.
POLONIUS: I will say so.

Exit.

HAMLET: By and by, is easily said. Leave me friends:

Exeunt all but Hamlet.

'Tis now the very witching time of night,
When churchyards yawn, and Hell itself breathes out
Contagion to this world. Now could I drink hot blood,
And do such bitter business as the day
Would quake to look on. Soft now, to my mother:
O heart, lose not thy nature; let not ever
The soul of Nero, enter this firm bosom:
Let me be cruel, not unnatural.
I will speak daggers to her, but use none:
My tongue and soul in this be hypocrites.
How in my words, somever she be shent,
To give them seals, never my soul consent.

Exit.

III.3

Enter King, Rosencrantz, and Guildenstern.

KING: I like him not, nor stands it safe with us,
To let his madness range. Therefore prepare you,
I your commission will forthwith dispatch,
And he to England shall along with you:
The terms of our estate, may not endure

Hazard so dangerous as doth hourly grow
Out of his lunacies.

GUILDENSTERN: We will ourselves provide:
Most holy and religious fear it is
To keep those many many bodies safe
That live and feed upon your Majesty.

ROSENCRANTZ: The single and peculiar life is bound
With all the strength and armour of the mind,
To keep itself fron noyance; but much more,
That spirit, upon whose weal depends and rests
The lives of many; the cease of Majesty
Dies not alone, but like a gulf doth draw
What's near it, with it. It is a massy wheel
Fix'd on the summit of the highest mount,
To whose huge spokes, ten thousand lesser things
Are mortis'd and adjoin'd: which when it falls,
Each small annexment, petty consequence
Attends the boisterous ruin. Never alone
Did the King sigh, but with a general groan.

KING: Arm you, I pray you to this speedy voyage;
For we will fetters put upon this fear,
Which now goes too free-footed

BOTH: We will haste us.

Exeunt

Enter Polonius.

POLONIUS: My Lord, he's going to his mother's closet:
Behind the arras I'll convey myself
To hear the process. I'll warrant she'll tax him home,
And as you said, and wisely was it said,
'Tis meet that some more audience than a mother,
Since Nature makes them partial, should o'erhear
The speech of vantage. Fare you well my Liege,
I'll call upon you ere you go to bed,
And tell you what I know,

KING: Thanks dear my Lord.

Exit Polonius.

Oh my offence is rank, it smells to Heaven,
It hath the primal eldest curse upon 't,
A brother's murther. Pray can I not,
Though inclination be as sharp as will:
My stronger guilt, defeats my strong intent,
And like a man to double business bound,
I stand in pause where I shall first begin,
And both neglect; what if this cursed hand
Were thicker than itself with brother's blood,
Is there not rain enough in the sweet heavens
To wash it white as snow? Whereto serves mercy,
But to confront the visage of offence?
And what's in prayer, but this twofold force,
To be forestalled ere we come to fall,
Or pardon'd being down? Then I'll look up,
My fault is past. But oh, what form of prayer
Can serve my turn? Forgive me my foul murther:
That cannot be, since I am still possess'd
Of those effects for which I did the murther,
My crown, mine own ambition, and my Queen.
May one be pardon'd, and retain th' offence?
In the corrupted currents of this world,
Offence's gilded hand may shove by Justice,
And oft 'tis seen, the wicked prize itself
Buys out the Law; but 'tis not so above,
There is no shuffling, there the action lies
In his true nature, and we ourselves compell'd
Even to the teeth and forehead of our faults,
To give in evidence. What then? what rests?
Try what repentance can. What can it not?
Yet what can it, when one cannot repent?

O wretched state! O bosom, black as death!
O limed soul, that struggling to be free,
Art more engag'd; help angels, make assay:
Bow stubborn knees, and heart with strings of steel,
Be soft as sinews of the new-born babe,
All may be well.

Enter Hamlet.

HAMLET: Now might I do it pat, now he is praying,
And now I'll do't, and so he goes to Heaven,
And so am I reveng'd: that would be scann'd,
A villain kills my father, and for that
I his sole son, do this same villain send
To Heaven.
O this is hire and salary, not revenge.
He took my father grossly, full of bread,
With all his crimes broad blown, as flush as May,
And how his audit stands, who knows, save Heaven:
But in our circumstance and course of thought
'Tis heavy with him; and am I then reveng'd,
To take him in the purging of his soul,
When he is fit and season'd for his passage?
No.
Up sword, and know thou a more horrid hent
When he is drunk asleep: or in his rage,
Or in th' incestuous pleasure of his bed,
At gaining, swearing, or about some act
That has no relish of salvation in't,
Then trip him, that his heels may kick at Heaven,
And that his soul may be as damn'd and black
As Hell, whereto it goes. My mother stays,
This physic but prolongs thy sickly days.

Exit.

KING: My words fly up, my thoughts remain below,
Words without thoughts, never to Heaven go.

III.4

Enter Queen and Polonius.

POLONIUS: He will come straight: look you lay home to him,
Tell him his pranks have been too broad to bear with,
And that your Grace hath screen'd, and stood between
Much heat, and him. I'll silence me e'en here:
Pray you be round with him.

HAMLET: Mother, mother, mother.

QUEEN: I'll warrant you, fear me not. Withdraw, I hear him coming.

Enter Hamlet.

HAMLET: Now mother, what's the matter?

QUEEN: Hamlet, thou hast thy father much offended.

HAMLET: Mother, you have my father much offended.

QUEEN: Come, come, you answer with an idle tongue.

HAMLET: Go, go, you question with an idle tongue.

QUEEN: Why how now Hamlet?

HAMLET: What's the matter now?

QUEEN: Have you forgot me?

HAMLET: No by the Rood, not so:
You are the Queen, your husband's brother's wife,
But would you were not so. You are my mother.

QUEEN: Nay, then I'll set those to you that can speak.

HAMLET: Come, come, and sit you down, you shall not budge:
You go not till I set you up a glass,
Where you may see the inmost part of you.

QUEEN: What wilt thou do? thou wilt not murder me?
Help, help, hoa.

POLONIUS: What hoa, help, help, help.

HAMLET: How now, a rat? dead for a ducat, dead.

Kills Polonius.

POLONIUS: O I am slain.
QUEEN: O me, what hast thou done?
HAMLET: Nay I know not, is it the King?
QUEEN: O what a rash, and bloody deed is this!
HAMLET: A bloody deed, almost as bad good mother,
    As kill a King, and marry with his brother.
QUEEN: As kill a King?
HAMLET: Ay Lady, 'twas my word.
    Thou wretched, rash, intruding fool, farewell.
    I took thee for thy better: take thy fortune,
    Thou find'st to be too busy, is some danger.
    Leave wringing of your hands, peace, sit you down,
    And let me wring your heart, for so I shall
    If it be made of penetrable stuff;
    If damned custom have not braz'd it so,
    That it is proof and bulwark against sense.
QUEEN: What have I done, that thou darest wag thy tongue
    In noise so rude against me?
HAMLET: Such an act
    That blurs the grace and blush of Modesty,
    Calls Virtue hypocrite, takes off the rose
    From the fair forehead of an innocent love,
    And sets a blister there, makes marriage-vows
    As false as dicers' oaths. O such a deed,
    As from the body of contraction plucks
    The very soul, and sweet Religion makes
    A rhapsody of words. Heaven's face doth glow,
    Yea this solidity and compound mass,
    With tristful visage as against the doom,
    Is thought-sick at the act.
QUEEN: Ay me; what act,
    That roars so loud, and thunders in the index?
HAMLET: Look here upon this picture, and on this,

The counterfeit presentment of two brothers:
See what a grace was seated on this brow,
Hyperion's curls, the front of Jove himself,
An eye like Mars, to threaten or command,
A station like the herald Mercury,
New-lighted on a heaven-kissing hill:
A combination, and a form indeed,
Where every god did seem to set his seal,
To give the world assurance of a man.
This was your husband. Look you now what follows.
Here is your husband, like a mildew'd ear
Blasting his wholesome breath. Have you eyes?
Could you on this fair mountain leave to feed,
And batten on this moor? Ha? have you eyes?
You cannot call it love: for at your age,
The hey-day in the blood is tame, it's humble,
And waits upon the judgement: and what judgement
Would step from this, to this? [Sense sure you have,
Else could you not have motion, but sure that sense
Is apoplex'd, for madness would not err,
Nor sense to ecstasy was ne'er so thrall'd
But it reserv'd some quantity of choice
To serve in such a difference.] What devil was't
That thus hath cozen'd you at hoodman-blind?
[Eyes without feeling, feeling without sights,
Eare without hands, or eyes, smelling, sans all,
Or but a sickly part of one true sense
Could not so mope.]
O Shame! where is thy blush? Rebellious Hell,
If thou canst mutine in a matron's bones,
To flaming youth, let virtue be as wax,
And melt in her own fire. Proclaim no shame,
When the compulsive ardour gives the charge,

Since frost itself, as actively doth burn
As Reason pandars Will.

QUEEN: O Hamlet, speak no more
Thou turn'st mine eyes into my very soul,
And there I see such black and grained spots,
As will not leave their tinct.

HAMLET: Nay, but to live,
In the rank sweat of an enseamed bed,
Stew'd in corruption; honeying and making love
Over the nasty sty.

QUEEN: O speak to me no more,
These words like daggers enter in mine ears.
No more sweet Hamlet.

HAMLET: A murderer, and a villain:
A slave, that is not twentieth part the tithe
Of your precedent Lord. A vice of Kings,
A cutpurse of the Empire and the rule,
That from a shelf, the precious diadem stole,
And put it in his pocket.

QUEEN: No more.

Enter Ghost.

HAMLET: A King of shreds and patches.
Save me; and hover o'er me with your wings
You heavenly guards. What would your gracious figure?

QUEEN: Alas he's mad.

HAMLET: Do you not come your tardy son to chide,
That laps'd in time and passion, lets go by
Th' important acting of your dread command?
Oh say.

GHOST: Do not forget: this visitation
Is but to whet thy almost blunted purpose.
But look, amazement on thy mother sits;
O step between her, and her fighting soul,

Conceit in weakest bodies, strongest works.
Speak to her Hamlet.
HAMLET: How is it with you Lady?
QUEEN: Alas, how is't with you?
That you bend your eye on vacancy,
And with the incorporal air do hold discourse.
Forth at your eyes your spirits wildly peep,
And as the sleeping soldiers in th' alarm,
Your bedded hair, like life in excrements,
Start up, and stand an end. Oh gentle son,
Upon the heat and flame of thy distemper
Sprinkle cool patience. Whereon do you look?
HAMLET: On him, on him: look you how pale he glares,
His form and cause conjoin'd, preaching to stones,
Would make them capable. Do not look upon me,
Lest with this piteous action you convert
My stern effects: then what I have to do,
Will want true colour; tears perchance for blood.
QUEEN: To whom do you speak this?
HAMLET: Do you see nothing there?
QUEEN: Nothing at all, yet all that is I see.
HAMLET: Nor did you nothing hear?
QUEEN: No, nothing but ourselves.
HAMLET: Why look you there: look how it steals away:
My father in his habit, as he lived,
Look where he goes even now out at the portal.

Exit Ghost.

QUEEN: This is the very coinage of your brain,
This bodiless creation ecstasy
Is very cunning in.
HAMLET: Ecstasy?
My pulse as yours doth temperately keep time,
And makes as healthful music. It is not madness

That I have uttered; bring me to the test
And I the matter will re-word, which madness
Would gambol from. Mother, for love of Grace,
Lay not a flattering unction to your soul,
That not your trespass, but my madness speaks:
It will but skin and film the ulcerous place,
Whilst rank corruption mining all within,
Infects unseen. Confess yourself to Heaven,
Repent what's past, avoid what is to come,
And do not spread the compost on the weeds,
To make them ranker. Forgive me this my virtue,
For in the fatness of these pursy times,
Virtue itself, of Vice must pardon beg,
Yea curb, and woo, for leave to do him good.

QUEEN: Oh Hamlet, Thou hast cleft my heart in twain.

HAMLET: O throw away the worser part of it,
And live the purer with the other half.
Good night, but go not to my uncle's bed,
Assume a virtue, if you have it not,
[That monster custom, who all sense doth eat
Of habits devil, is angel yet in this,
That to the use of actions fair and good,
He likewise gives a frock or livery
That aptly is put on.] Refrain to-night;
And that shall lend a kind of easiness
To the next abstinence. [The next more easy;
For use almost can change the stamp of nature,
And either the devil, or throw him out
With wondrous potency.] Once more good night,
And when you are desirous to be blest,
I'll blessing beg of you. For this same Lord,
I do repent: but Heaven hath pleas'd it so,
To punish me with this, and this with me,

That I must be their scourge and minister.
I will bestow him, and will answer well
The death I gave him: so again, good night.
I must be cruel, only to be kind;
Thus bad begins and worse remains behind.
[One word more good lady.]

QUEEN: What shall I do?

HAMLET: Not this by no means that I bid you do:
Let the bloat King tempt you again to bed,
Pinch wanton on your cheek, call you his mouse,
And let him for a pair of reechy kisses,
Or paddling in your neck with his damn'd fingers,
Make you to ravel all this matter out,
That I essentially am not in madness,
But mad in craft. 'Twere good you let him know,
For who that's but a Queen, fair, sober, wise,
Would from a paddock, from a bat, a gib,
Such dear concerning hide? who would do so?
No, in despite of sense and secrecy,
Unpeg the basket on the house's top,
Let the birds fly, and like the famous ape
To try conclusions in the basket, creep
And break your own neck down.

QUEEN: Be thou assur'd, if words be made of breath,
And breath of life: I have no life to breathe
What thou hast said to me.

HAMLET: I must to England, you know that?

QUEEN: Alack
I had forgot: 'tis so concluded on.

HAMLET: [There's letters seal'd, and my two school-fellows,
Whom I will trust as I will adders fang'd,
They bear the mandate, they must sweep my way
And marshal me to knavery: let it work,

For 'tis the sport to have the enginer
Hoist with his own petar, and 't shall go hard
But I will delve one yard below their mines,
And blow them at the moon: O 'tis most sweet
When in one line two crafts directly meet.]
This man shall set me packing:
I'll lug the guts into the neighbour room;
Mother good night. Indeed this Councillor
Is now most still, most secret, and most grave,
Who was in life, a foolish prating knave.
Come sir, to draw toward an end with you.
Good night, mother.

Exit Hamlet tugging in Polonius.

IV.1

Enter King.

KING: There's matter in these sighs. These profound heaves
You must translate; 'tis fit we understand them.
Where is your son?
QUEEN: Ah mine own Lord, what have I seen to-night!
KING: What Gertrude? How does Hamlet?
QUEEN: Mad as the seas, and wind, when both contend
Which is the mightier: in his lawless fit
Behind the arras, hearing something stir,
He whips out his rapier, and cries A rat, a rat,
And in this brainish apprehension kills
The unseen good old man.
KING: O heavy deed:
It had been so with us had we been there:
His liberty is full of threats to all,

To you yourself, to us, to every one.
Alas, how shall this bloody deed be answer'd?
It will be laid to us, whose providence
Should have kept short, restrain'd, and out of haunt
This mad young man. But so much was our love,
We would not understand what was most fit,
But like the owner of a foul disease,
To keep it from divulging, lets it feed
Even on the pith of life. Where is he gone?

QUEEN: To draw apart the body he hath kill'd,
O'er whom his very madness like some ore
Among a mineral of metals base
Shows itself pure. He weeps for what is done.

KING: O Gertrude, come away:
The sun no sooner shall the mountains touch,
But we will ship him hence, and this vile deed,
We must with all our majesty and skill
Both countenance, and excuse. Ho Guildenstern:

Enter Rosencrantz and Guildenstern.

Friends both go join you with some further aid:
Hamlet in madness hath Polonius slain,
And from his mother's closet hath he dragg'd him.
Go seek him out, speak fair, and bring the body
Into the Chapel. I pray you haste in this.

Exeunt Rosencrantz and Guildenstern.

Come Gertrude, we'll call up our wisest friends,
To let them know both what we mean to do,
And what's untimely done
[Whose whisper o'er the world's diameter,
As level as the cannon to his blank,
Transports his poison'd shot, may miss our name,
And hit the woundless air]. O come away.
My soul is full of discord and dismay.

Exeunt.

IV.2

Enter Hamlet.

HAMLET: Safely stowed.

ROSENCRANTZ / GUILDENSTERN: [*Within*] Hamlet, Lord Hamlet.

HAMLET: What noise? Who calls on Hamlet? O here they come.

Enter Rosencrantz and Guildenstern.

ROSENCRANTZ: What have you done my Lord with the dead body ?

HAMLET: Compounded it with dust, whereto 'tis kin.

ROSENCRANTZ: Tell us where 'tis, that we may take it thence,
And bear it to the Chapel.

HAMLET: Do not believe it.

ROSENCRANTZ: Believe what?

HAMLET: That I can keep your counsel, and not mine own. Besides, to be demanded of a sponge, what replication should be made by the son of a King?

ROSENCRANTZ: Take you me for a sponge, my Lord?

HAMLET: Ay sir, that soaks up the King's countenance, his rewards, his authorities. But such officers do the King best service in the end. He keeps them like an ape in the corner of his jaw, first mouth'd to be last swallowed, when he needs what you have glean'd, it is but squeezing you, and sponge you shall be dry again.

ROSENCRANTZ: I understand you not my Lord.

HAMLET: I am glad of it: a knavish speech sleeps in a foolish ear.

ROSENCRANTZ: My Lord, you must tell us where the body is, and go with us to the King.

HAMLET: The body is with the King, but the King is not with the body. The King is a thing–

GUILDENSTERN: A thing my Lord?

HAMLET: Of nothing: bring me to him, hide fox, and all after.

Exeunt.

IV.3

Enter King.

KING: I have sent to seek him, and to find the body:
How dangerous is it that this man goes loose:
Yet must not we put the strong Law on him:
He's loved of the distracted multitude,
Who like not in their judgement, but their eyes:
And where 'tis so, th' offender's scourge is weigh'd
But never the offence: to bear all smooth, and even,
This sudden sending him away, must seem
Deliberate pause; diseases desperate grown,
By desperate appliance are relieved,
Or not at all.

Enter Rosencrantz.

How now? what hath befall'n?

ROSENCRANTZ: Where the dead body is bestow'd my Lord,
We cannot get from him.

KING: But where is he?

ROSENCRANTZ: Without my Lord, guarded to know your pleasure.

KING: Bring him before us.

ROSENCRANTZ: Hoa, Guildenstern! Bring in my Lord.

Enter Hamlet and Guildenstern.

KING: Now Hamlet, where's Polonius?

HAMLET: At supper.

KING: At supper? Where?

HAMLET: Not where he eats, but where he is eaten, a certain convocation of politic worms are e'en at him. Your worm is your only Emperor for diet. We fat all creatures else to fat us, and we fat ourselves for maggots. Your fat King and your lean beggar, is but variable service, two dishes but to one table; that's the end.

[KING: Alas, alas.

HAMLET: A man may fish with the worm that hath eat of a King, and eat of the fish that hath fed of that worm.]

KING: What dost thou mean by this?

HAMLET: Nothing but to show you how a King may go a progress through the guts of a beggar.

KING: Where is Polonius?

HAMLET: In heaven, send hither to see. If your messenger find him not there, seek him i' th' other place yourself: but indeed, if you find him not within this month, you shall nose him as you go up the stairs into the lobby.

KING: Go seek him there.

HAMLET: He will stay till ye come.

KING: Hamlet, this deed for thine especial safety,
Which we do tender, as we dearly grieve
For that which thou hast done, must send thee hence
With fiery quickness. Therefore prepare thyself,
The bark is ready, and the wind at help,
Th' associates tend, and every thing is bent
For England.

HAMLET: For England?

KING: Ay Hamlet.

HAMLET: Good.

KING: So is it, if thou knew'st our purposes.

HAMLET: I see a cherub that sees them: but come, for England.
Farewell dear mother.

KING: Thy loving father Hamlet.

HAMLET: My mother: father and mother is man and wife; man and wife is one flesh, and so my mother. Come, for England.

Exit.

KING: Follow him at foot, tempt him with speed aboard:
Delay it not, I'll have him hence to-night.
Away, for every thing is seal'd and done
That else leans on th' affair; pray you make haste.
And England, if my love thou hold'st at aught,
As my great power thereof may give thee sense,
Since yet thy cicatrice looks raw and red
After the Danish sword, and thy free awe
Pays homage to us; thou mayst not coldly set
Our sovereign process, which imports at full
By letters conjuring to that effect
The present death of Hamlet. Do it England,
For like the hectic in my blood he rages,
And thou must cure me; till I know 'tis done,
Howe'er my haps, my joys were ne'er begun.

Exit.

IV.4

Enter Fortinbras with his army over the stage.

FORTINBRAS: Go Captain, from me greet the Danish King,
Tell him, that by his license Fortinbras
Craves the conveyance of a promis'd march
Over his Kingdom. You know the rendezvous:
If that his Majesty would aught with us,
We shall express our duty in his eye,
And let him know so.

CAPTAIN: I will do't my Lord.
FORTINBRAS: Go softly on.

Exeunt Fortinbras and Soldiers.
[Enter Hamlet, Rosencrantz, and others.

HAMLET: Good sir whose powers are these?
CAPTAIN: They are of Norway sir.
HAMLET: How purpos'd sir I pray you?
CAPTAIN: Against some part of Poland.
HAMLET: Who commands them sir?
CAPTAIN: The nephew to old Norway, Fortinbras.
HAMLET: Goes it against the main of Poland sir,
Or for some frontier?
CAPTAIN: Truly to speak, and with no addition,
We go to gain a little patch of ground
That hath in it no profit but the name:
To pay five ducats, five I would not farm it;
Nor will it yield to Norway or the Pole
A ranker rate, should it be sold in fee.
HAMLET: Why then the Polack never will defend it
CAPTAIN: Yes, it is already garrison'd.
HAMLET: Two thousand souls, and twenty thousand ducats
Will not debate the question of this straw.
This is th' imposthume of much wealth and peace,
That inward breaks, and shows no cause without
Why the man dies. I humbly thank you sir.
CAPTAIN: God buy you, sir.

Exit.

ROSENCRANTZ: Will't please you go my Lord?
HAMLET: I'll be with you straight, go a little before.

Exeunt all but Hamlet.

How all occasions do inform against me,
And spur my dull revenge. What is a man
If his chief good and market of his time

Be but to sleep and feed? a beast, no more:
Sure he that made us with such large discourse
Looking before and after, gave us not
That capability and god-like reason
To fust in us unus'd. Now whether it be
Bestial oblivion, or some craven scruple
Of thinking too precisely on th' event,
A thought which quarter'd hath but one part wisdom,
And ever three parts coward, I do not know
Why yet I live to say This thing's to do,
Sith I have cause, and will, and strength, and means
To do't; examples gross as earth exhort me,
Witness this army of such mass and charge,
Led by a delicate and tender Prince,
Whose spirit with divine ambition puff'd,
Makes mouths at the invisible event,
Exposing what is mortal, and unsure,
To all that fortune, death, and danger dare,
Even for an egg-shell. Rightly to be great,
Is not to stir without great argument,
But greatly to find quarrel in a straw
When honour's at the stake. How stand I then
That have a father kill'd, a mother stain'd,
Excitements of my reason, and my blood,
And let all sleep, while to my shame I see
The imminent death of twenty thousand men,
That for a fantasy and trick of fame
Go to their graves like beds, fight for a plot
Whereon the numbers cannot try the cause,
Which is not tomb enough and continent
To hide the slain? O from this time forth,
My thoughts be bloody, or be nothing worth.]

Exit.

IV.5

Enter Queen and Horatio.

QUEEN: I will not speak with her.
HORATIO: She is importunate, indeed distract,
Her mood will needs be pitied.
QUEEN: What would she have?
HORATIO: She speaks much of her father; says she hears
There's tricks i' th' world, and hems, and beats her heart,
Spurns enviously at straws, speaks things in doubt,
That carry but half sense; her speech is nothing,
Yet the unshaped use of it doth move
The hearers to collection; they aim at it,
And botch the words up fit to their own thoughts,
Which as her winks, and nods, and gestures yield them,
Indeed would make one think there might be thought,
Though nothing sure, yet much unhappily.
QUEEN: 'Twere good she were spoken with, for she may strew
Dangerous conjectures in ill-breeding minds.
Let her come in.
To my sick soul (as sin's true nature is)
Each toy seems prologue, to some great amiss:
So full of artless jealousy is guilt,
It spills itself, in fearing to be spilt.

Enter Ophelia, distracted.

OPHELIA: Where is the beauteous Majesty of Denmark?
QUEEN: How now Ophelia?
OPHELIA:

She Sings.

How should I your true love know
From another one?
By his cockle hat and staff,
And his sandal shoon.

QUEEN: Alas sweet Lady: what imports this song?

OPHELIA: Say you? nay pray you mark.

He is dead and gone Lady,
He is dead and gone,
At his head a grass-green turf,
At his heels a stone.

Enter King.

QUEEN: Nay but Ophelia.

OPHELIA: Pray you mark.

White his shroud as the mountain snow.

QUEEN: Alas, look here my Lord.

OPHELIA:

Larded with sweet flowers:
Which bewept to the grave did not go
With true-love showers.

KING: How do ye, pretty Lady?

OPHELIA: Well, God 'ild you. They say the owl was a baker's daughter. Lord, we know what we are, but know not what we may be. God be at your table.

KING: Conceit upon her father.

OPHELIA: Pray you let's have no words of this: but when they ask you what it means, say you this:

To-morrow is Saint Valentine's day,
All in the morning betime,
And I a maid at your window,
To be your Valentine.
Then up he rose, and donn'd his clothes,
And dupped the chamber door,
Let in the maid, that out a maid
Never departed more.

KING: Pretty Ophelia.

OPHELIA: Indeed la, without an oath I'll make an end on't

By Gis, and by Saint Charity,
Alack, and fie for shame:
Young men will do't, if they come to 't,
By Cock they are to blame.
Quoth she, before you tumbled me,
You promis'd me to wed.
So would I ha' done by yonder sun,
And thou hadst not come to my bed.

KING: How long hath she been thus?

OPHELIA: I hope all will be well. We must be patient, but I cannot choose but weep, to think they should lay him i' th' cold ground: my brother shall know of it, and so I thank you for your good counsel. Come, my coach: good night Ladies: good night sweet Ladies: good night, good night.

Exit.

KING: Follow her close, give her good watch I pray you:

Exit Horatio.

O this is the poison of deep grief, it springs
All from her father's death. O Gertrude, Gertrude,
When sorrows come, they come not single spies,
But in battalions. First, her father slain,
Next your son gone, and he most violent author
Of his own just remove: the people muddied,
Thick and unwholesome in their thoughts, and whispers
For good Polonius' death; and we have done but greenly
In hugger-mugger to inter him. Poor Ophelia
Divided from herself, and her fur judgement,
Without the which we are pictures, or mere beasts.
Last, and as much containing as all these,
Her brother is in secret come from France,
Feeds on his wonder, keeps himself in clouds,
And wants not buzzers to infect his ear
With pestilent speeches of his father's death,

Wherein necessity of matter beggar'd,
Will nothing stick our persons to arraign
In ear and ear. O my dear Gertrude, this,
Like to a murdering-piece in many places,
Gives me superfluous death.

A noise within. Enter a Messenger.

QUEEN: Alack, what noise is this?

KING: Where are my Switzers? Let them guard the door.
What is the matter?

MESSENGER: Save yourself, my Lord.
The ocean (overpeering of his list)
Eats not the flats with more impiteous haste
Than young Laertes, in a riotous head,
O'erbears your officers, the rabble call him Lord,
And as the world were now but to begin,
Antiquity forgot, custom not known,
The ratifiers and props of every word,
They cry Choose we! Laertes shall be King,
Caps, hands, and tongues, applaud it to the clouds,
Laertes shall be King, Laertes King.

QUEEN: How cheerfully on the false trail they cry.
O this is counter you false Danish dogs.

Noise within.

KING: The doors are broke.

Enter Laertes with others.

LAERTES: Where is this King, sirs? stand you all without.

ALL: No, let's come in.

LAERTES: I pray you give me leave.

ALL: We will, we will.

Exeunt.

LAERTES: I thank you: keep the door. O thou vile King, Give me my father.

QUEEN: Calmly good Laertes.
LAERTES: That drop of blood that's calm proclaims me bastard,
Cries cuckold to my father, brands the harlot
Even here, between the chaste unsmirched brow
Of my true mother.
KING: What is the cause Laertes,
That thy rebellion looks so giant-like?
Let him go Gertrude: do not fear our person:
There's such divinity doth hedge a King,
That Treason can but peep to what it would,
Acts little of his will. Tell me Laertes,
Why thou art thus incensed? Let him go Gertrude.
Speak man.
LAERTES: Where is my father?
KING: Dead.
QUEEN: But not by him.
KING: Let him demand his fill.
LAERTES: How came he dead? I'll not be juggl'd with.
To hell allegiance: vows, to the blackest devil.
Conscience and grace, to the profoundest pit.
I dare damnation: to this point I stand,
That both the worlds I give to negligence,
Let come what comes: only I'll be reveng'd
Most throughly for my father.
KING: Who shall stay you?
LAERTES: My will, not all the world;
And for my means, I'll husband them so well,
They shall go far with little.
KING: Good Laertes:
If you desire to know the certainty
Of your dear father's death, is't writ in your revenge,
That swoopstake you will draw both friend and foe,
Winner and loser?
LAERTES: None but his enemies.

KING: Will you know them then?

LAERTES: To his good friends, thus wide I'll ope my arms:
And like the kind life-rendering pelican,
Repast them with my blood.

KING: Why now you speak
Like a good child, and a true gentleman.
That I am guiltless of your father's death,
And am most sensibly in grief for it,
It shall as level to your judgement pierce
As day does to your eye.

A noise within: 'Let her come in'.
Enter Ophelia.

LAERTES: How now? what noise is that?
O heat dry up my brains, tears seven times salt,
Burn out the sense and virtue of mine eye.
By Heaven, thy madness shall be paid by weight,
Till our scale turns the beam. O Rose of May,
Dear maid, kind sister, sweet Ophelia:
O Heavens, is't possible a young maid's wits
Should be as mortal as an old man's life?
Nature is fine in love, and where 'tis fine,
It sends some precious instance of itself
After the thing it loves.

OPHELIA: *Sings.*
They bore him barefac'd on the bier,
Hey non nonny, nonny, hey nonny;
And on his grave rain'd many a tear,

Fare you well my dove.

LAERTES: Hadst thou thy wits, and didst persuade revenge,
It could not move thus.

OPHELIA: You must sing down a-down,
An you call him a-down-a.
Oh, how the wheel becomes it! It is the false steward that stole his master's daughter.

LAERTES: This nothing's more than matter.

OPHELIA: There's rosemary, that's for remembrance. Pray love remember: and there is pansies, that's for thoughts.

LAERTES: A document in madness, thoughts and remembrance fitted.

OPHELIA: There's fennel for you, and columbines: there's rue for you, and here's some for me. We may call it herb of grace a' Sundays: Oh you must wear your rue with a difference. There's a daisy, I would give you some violets, but they wither'd all when my father died: they say, he made a good end;

For bonny sweet Robin is all my joy.

LAERTES: Thought, and affliction, passion, hell itself,
She turns to favour, and to prettiness.

OPHELIA: *And will he not come again,*
And will he not come again?
No, no, he is dead,
Go to thy death-bed,
He never will come again,
His bear was as white as snow,
All flaxen was his poll:
He is gone, he is gone,
And we cast away moan,
Gramercy on his soul,
And of all Christian souls, I pray God. God buy ye.

Exit Ophelia.

LAERTES: Do you see this, O God?

KING: Laertes, I must commune with your grief,
Or you deny me right: go but apart,
Make choice of whom your wisest friends you will,
And they shall hear and judge 'twixt you and me;
If by direct or by collateral hand
They find us touch'd, we will our Kingdom give,

Our Crown, our life, and all that we call ours
To you in satisfaction. But if not,
Be you content to lend your patience to us,
And we shall jointly labour with your soul
To give it due content.

LAERTES: Let this be so:
His means of death, his obscure burial,
No trophy, sword, nor hatchment o'er his bones,
No noble rite, nor formal ostentation,
Cry to be heard, as 'twere from Heaven to Earth,
That I must call in question.

KING: So you shall:
And where th' offence is, let the great axe fall.
I pray you go with me.

Exeunt.

IV.6

Enter Horatio, with an Attendant.

HORATIO: What are they that would speak with me?

ATTENDANT: Sailors, sir, they say they have letters for you.

HORATIO: Let them come in,
I do not know from what part of the world
I should be greeted, if not from Lord Hamlet.

Enter Sailor.

SAILOR: God bless you sir.

HORATIO: Let him bless thee too.

SAILOR: He shall sir, and please him. There's a letter for you sir: it comes from th' ambassadors that was bound for England, if your name be Horatio, as I am let to know it is.

HORATIO reads the letter: *Horatio, when thou shalt have o'erlooked this, give these fellows some means to die King; they have letters for him. Ere we were two days old at sea, a pirate of very warlike appointment gave us chase. Finding ourselves too slow of sail, we put on a compelled valour. In the grapple, I boarded them: on the instant they got clear of our ship, so I alone became their prisoner. They have dealt with me, like thieves of mercy, but they knew what they did. I am to do a good turn for them. Let the King have the letters I have sent, and repair thou to me with as much haste as thou wouldst fly death. I have words to speak in your ear, will make thee dumb, yet are they much too light for the bore of the matter. These good fellows will bring thee where I am. Rosencrantz and Guildenstern hold their course for England. Of them I have much to tell thee, farewell. He that thou knowest thine,*
HAMLET.
Come, I will give way for these your letters,
And do't the speedier, that you may direct me
To him from whom you brought them.

Exeunt.

IV.7

Enter King and Laertes.

KING: Now must your conscience my acquittance seal,
And you must put me in your heart for friend,
Sith you have heard, and with a knowing ear,
That he which hath your noble father slain,
Pursued my life.

LAERTES: It well appears. But tell me,
Why you proceeded not against these feats,
So crimeful, and so capital in nature,
As by your safety, wisdom, all things else,
You mainly were stirr'd up.
KING: O for two special reasons,
Which may to you (perhaps) seem much unsinew'd,
And yet to me they are strong. The Queen his mother,
Lives almost by his looks: and for myself,
My virtue or my plague, be it either which,
She's so conjunctive to my life and soul,
That as the star moves not but in his sphere,
I could not but by her. The other motive,
Why to a public count I might not go,
Is the great love the general gender bear him,
Who dipping all his faults in their affection,
Would like the spring that turneth wood to stone,
Convert his gyves to graces. So that my arrows
Too slightly timber'd for so loud a wind,
Would have reverted to my bow again,
And not where I had aim'd them.
LAERTES: And so have I a noble father lost,
A sister driven into desperate terms,
Whose worth (if praises may go back again)
Stood challenger on mount of all the age
For her perfections. But my revenge will come.
KING: Break not your sleeps for that, you must not think
That we are made of stuff, so flat, and dull,
That we can let our beard be shook with danger,
And think it pastime. You shortly shall hear more,
I lov'd your father, and we love ourself,
And that I hope will teach you to imagine—

Enter a Messenger.

How now? What news?

MESSENGER: Letters my Lord from Hamlet.
This to your Majesty: this to the Queen.
KING: From Hamlet? Who brought them?
MESSENGER: Sailors my Lord they say, I saw them not: They were given to me by Claudio, he receiv'd them of him that brought them.
KING: Laertes you shall hear them:
Leave us.

Exit Messenger.

High and Mighty, You shall know I am set naked on your Kingdom. To-morrow shall I beg leave to see your kingly eyes. When I shall (first asking your pardon thereunto) recount the occasions of my sudden and more strange return.

HAMLET

What should this mean? Are all the rest come back?
Or is it some abuse? or no such thing?
LAERTES: Know you the hand?
KING: 'Tis Hamlet's character. Naked,
And in a postscript here he says alone:
Can you advise me?
LAERTES: I'm lost in it my Lord; but let him come,
It warms the very sickness in my heart,
That I shall live and tell him to his teeth;
Thus didest thou.
KING: If it be so Laertes,
As how should it be so, how otherwise,
Will you be rul'd by me?
LAERTES: If so you'll not o'errule me to a peace.
KING: To thine own peace: if he be now return'd,
As checking at his voyage, and that he means
No more to undertake it; I will work him
To an exploit now ripe in my device,
Under the which he shall not choose but fall:
And for his death no wind of blame shall breathe,

But even his mother shall uncharge the practice,
And call it accident.
[LAERTES: My Lord I will be ruled,
The rather if you could devise it so
That I might be die organ.
KING: It falls right,
You have been talk'd of since your travel much,
And that in Hamlet's hearing, for a quality
Wherein they say you shine, your sum of parts
Did not together pluck such envy from him
As did that one, and that in my regard
Of the unworthiest siege.
LAERTES: What part is that my Lord?
KING: A very riband in the cap of youth,
Yet needful too, for youth no less becomes
The light and careless livery that it wears
Than settled age, his sables, and his weeds,
Importing health and graveness.] Some two months hence,
Here was a gentleman of Normandy,
I've seen myself, and serv'd against the French,
And they can well on horseback; but this gallant
Had witchcraft in't; he grew into his seat,
And to such wondrous doing brought his horse,
As he had been incorps'd and demi-natur'd
With the brave beast, so far he pass'd my thought,
That I in forgery of shapes and tricks,
Come short of what he did.
LAERTES: A Norman was't?
KING: A Norman.
LAERTES: Upon my life Lamound.
KING: The very same.
LAERTES: I know him well, he is the brooch indeed,
And gem of all the nation.
KING: He made confession of you,
And gave you such a masterly report,
For art and exercise in your defence;

And for your rapier most especially,
That he cried out, 'twould be a sight indeed,
If one could match you [the scrimers of their nation
He swore had neither motion, guard nor eye,
If you oppos'd them;] sir, this report of his
Did Hamlet so envenom with his envy,
That he could nothing do but wish and beg,
Your sudden coming o'er to play with him;
Now out of this.

LAERTES: What out of this, my Lord?

KING: Laertes was your father dear to you?
Or are you like the painting of a sorrow,
A face without a heart?

LAERTES: Why ask you this?

KING: Not that I think you did not love your father,
But that I know Love is begun by Time:
And that I see in passages of proof,
Time qualifies the spark and fire of it:
[There lives within the very flame of love
A kind of wick or snuff that will abate it,
And nothing is at a like goodness still,
For goodness growing to a plurisy,
Dies in his own too much; that we would do.
We should do when we would: for this would changes
And hath abatements and delays as many,
As there are tongues, are hands, are accidents,
And then this should is like a spendthrift's sigh,
That hurts by easing; but, to the quick of th' ulcer,]
Hamlet comes back: what would you undertake,
To show yourself your father's son indeed,
More than in words?

LAERTES: To cut his throat i' th' Church.

KING: No place indeed should murder sanctuarize;
Revenge should have no bounds: but good Laertes
Will you do this, keep close within your chamber,

Hamlet return'd, shall know you are come home:
We'll put on those shall praise your excellence,
And set a double varnish on the fame
The Frenchman gave you, bring you in fine together,
And wager on your heads ; he being remiss,
Most generous, and free from all contriving,
Will not peruse the foils! so that with ease,
Or with a little shuffling, you may choose
A sword unbated, and in a pass of practice,
Requite him for your father.

LAERTES: I will do't,
And for that purpose I'll anoint my sword:
I bought an unction of a mountebank
So mortal, that but dip a knife in it,
Where it draws blood, no cataplasm so rare,
Collected from all simples that have virtue
Under the Moon, can save the thing from death,
That is but scratch'd withal: I'll touch my point,
With this contagion, that if I gall him slightly,
It may be death.

KING: Let's further think of this,
Weigh what convenience both of time and means
May fit us to our shape, if this should fail;
And that our drift look through our bad performance,
'Twere better not assay'd; therefore this project
Should have a back or second, that might hold,
If this should blast in proof: soft, let me see,
We'll make a solemn wager on your cunnings,
I ha't:
When in your motion you are hot and dry,
As make your bouts more violent to that end,
And that he calls for drink; I'll have prepar'd him
A chalice for the nonce; whereon but sipping,
If he by chance escape your venom'd stuck,

Our purpose may hold there;
How sweet Queen.

Enter Queen.

QUEEN: One woe doth tread upon another's heel,
So fast they follow: your sister's drown'd, Laertes.
LAERTES: Drown'd! O where?
QUEEN: There is a willow grows aslant a brook,
That shows his hoar leaves in the glassy stream:
There with fantastic garlands did she come,
Of crow-flowers, nettles, daisies, and long purples,
That liberal shepherds give a grosser name;
But our cold maids do dead men's fingers call them:
There on the pendent boughs, her coronet weeds
Clambering to hang; an envious sliver broke,
When down her weedy trophies, and herself
Fell in the weeping brook; her clothes spread wide,
And mermaid-like, awhile they bore her up,
Which time she chanted snatches of old tunes,
As one incapable of her own distress,
Or like a creature native, and indued
Unto that element: but long it could not be,
Till that her garments, heavy with their drink,
Pull'd the poor wretch from her melodious lay,
To muddy death.
LAERTES: Adas then, she is drown'd?
QUEEN: Drown'd, drown'd.
LAERTES: Too much of water hast thou poor Ophelia,
And therefore I forbid my tears: but yet
It is our trick, Nature her custom holds,
Let shame say what it will; when these are gone.
The woman will be out: adieu my Lord,
I have a speech of fire, that fain would blaze,
But that this folly douts it.

Exit.

KING: Let's follow, Gertrude:
How much I had to do to calm his rage!
Now fear I this will give it start again;
Therefore let's follow.

Exeunt.

V.I

Enter two Clowns.

FIRST CLOWN: Is she to be buried in Christian burial, that wilfully seeks her own salvation?

SECOND CLOWN: I tell thee she is, and therefore make her grave straight, the crowner hath sat on her, and finds it Christian burial.

FIRST CLOWN: How can that be, unless she drowned herself in her own defence?

SECOND CLOWN: Why, 'tis found so.

FIRST CLOWN: It must be *se offendendo*, it cannot be else: for here lies the point; if I drown myself wittingly, it argues an act: and an act hath three branches; it is to act, to do, and to perform; argal she drown'd herself wittingly.

SECOND CLOWN: Nay but hear you goodman delver.

FIRST CLOWN: Give me leave; here lies the water; good: here stands the man; good; if the man go to this water and drown himself; it is will he nill he, he goes; mark you that? but if the water come to him and drown him, he drowns not himself. Argal, he that is not guilty of his own death, shortens not his own life.

SECOND CLOWN: But is this law?

FIRST CLOWN: Ay marry is't, crowner's Quest Law.

SECOND CLOWN: Will you ha' the truth on't: if this had not been a gentlewoman, she should have been buried out of Christian burial.

FIRST CLOWN: Why there thou say'st. And the more pity that great folk should have countenance in this world to drown or hang themselves, more than their even Christian. Come, my spade; there is no ancient gentlemen, but gardeners, ditchers and grave-makers; they hold up Adam's profession.

SECOND CLOWN: Was he a gentleman?

FIRST CLOWN: He was the first that ever bore arms.

SECOND CLOWN: Why he had none.

FIRST CLOWN: What, art a heathen? How dost thou understand the Scripture? The Scripture says Adam digg'd; could he dig without arms? I'll put another question to thee; if thou answerest me not to the purpose, confess thyself—

SECOND CLOWN: Go to.

FIRST CLOWN: What is he that builds stronger than either the mason, the shipwright, or the carpenter?

SECOND CLOWN: The gallows-maker; for that frame outlives a thousand tenants.

FIRST CLOWN: I like thy wit well in good faith, the gallows does well; but how does it well? it does well to those that do ill: now, thou dost ill to say the gallows is built stronger than the church: argal, the gallows may do well to thee. To't again, come.

SECOND CLOWN: Who builds stronger than a mason, a shipwright, or a carpenter?

FIRST CLOWN: Ay, tell me that, and unyoke.

SECOND CLOWN: Marry, now I can tell.

FIRST CLOWN: To't.

SECOND CLOWN: Mass, I cannot tell.

Enter Hamlet and Horatio afar off.

FIRST CLOWN: Cudgel thy brains no more about it; for your dull ass will not mend his pace with beating; and when you are ask'd this question next, say a grave-maker: the houses that he makes, last till Doomsday: go, get thee to Yaughan, fetch me a stoup of liquor.

Exit Second Clown.

Sings

In youth when I did love, did love
Methought it was very sweet:
To contract O the time for a my behove,
O methought there was nothing meet.

HAMLET: Has this fellow no feelings of his business, that he sings at grave-making?

HORATIO: Custom hath made it in him a property of easiness.

HAMLET: 'Tis e'en so; the hand of little employment hath the daintier sense.

FIRST CLOWN: *Sings*

But Age with his stealing steps
Hath claw'd me in his clutch:
And hath shipped me intil the land,
As if I had never been such.

HAMLET: That skull had a tongue in it, and could sing once: how the knave jowls it to th' ground, as if it were Cain's jaw-bone, that did the first murther: it might be the pate of a politician which this ass now o'er-reaches: one that would circumvent God, might it not?

HORATIO: It might, my Lord.

HAMLET: Or of a courtier, which could say, Good-morrow sweet Lord: how dost thou, good Lord? This might be my Lord such-a-one, that prais'd my Lord such- a-one's horse, when he meant to beg it; might it not?

HORATIO: Ay, my Lord.

HAMLET: Why e'en so: and now my Lady Worm's, chapless, and knocked about the mazzard with a sexton's spade; here's fine revolution, if we had the trick to see't.

Did these bones cost no more the breeding, but to play at loggats with 'em? mine ache to think on't.

FIRST CLOWN: *Sings*

A pick-haxe and a spade, a spade,
For and a shrouding sheet:

O a pit of clay for to be made,
For such a guest is meet.

HAMLET: There's another: why might not that be the skull of a lawyer? Where be his quiddits now? his quillets? his cases? his tenures, and his tricks? why does he suffer this rude knave now to knock him about the sconce with a dirty shovel, and will not tell him of his action of battery? Hum. This fellow might be in's time a great buyer of land, with his statutes, his recognizances, his fines, his double vouchers, his recoveries: is this the fine of his fines, and the recovery of his recoveries, to have his fine pate full of fine dirt? will his vouchers vouch him no more of his purchases, and double ones too, than the length and breadth of a pair of indentures? The very conveyances of his lands will hardly lie in this box; and must the inheritor himself have no more? ha?

HORATIO: Not a jot more my Lord.

HAMLET: Is not parchment made of sheep-skins?

HORATIO: Ay my Lord, and of calf-skins too.

HAMLET: They are sheep and calves that seek out assurance in that. I will speak to this fellow: whose grave's this sir?

FIRST CLOWN: Mine sir:

O a pit of clay for to be made,
For such a guest is meet.

HAMLET: I think it be thine indeed: for thou liest in't.

FIRST CLOWN: You lie out on't sir, and therefore 'tis not yours: for my part, I do not lie in't; and yet it is mine.

HAMLET: Thou dost lie in't to be in't and say it is thine: 'tis for the dead, not for the quick, therefore thou liest.

FIRST CLOWN: 'Tis a quick lie sir, 'twill away again from me to you.

HAMLET: What man dost thou dig it for?

FIRST CLOWN: For no man sir.

HAMLET: What woman then?

FIRST CLOWN: For none neither.

HAMLET: Who is to be buried in't?

FIRST CLOWN: One that was a woman sir; but rest her soul, she's dead.

HAMLET: How absolute the knave is! we must speak by the card, or equivocation will undo us. By the Lord Horatio, this three years I have taken note of it, the age is grown so picked, that the toe of the peasant comes so near the heel of our courtier, he galls his kibe. How long hast thou been a grave-maker?

FIRST CLOWN: Of all the days i' th' year, I came to't that day that our last King Hamlet o'ercame Fortinbras.

HAMLET: How long is that since?

FIRST CLOWN: Cannot you tell that? every fool can tell that: it was the very day that young Hamlet was born, he that is mad, and sent into England.

HAMLET: Ay marry, why was he sent into England?

FIRST CLOWN: Why, because he was mad; he shall recover his wits there; or if he do not, it's no great matter there.

HAMLET: Why?

FIRST CLOWN: 'Twill not be seen in him there, there the men are as mad as he.

HAMLET: How came he mad?

FIRST CLOWN: Very strangely they say.

HAMLET: How strangely?

FIRST CLOWN: Faith e'en with losing his wits.

HAMLET: Upon what ground?

FIRST CLOWN: Why here in Denmark: I have been sexton here, man and boy thirty years.

HAMLET: How long will a man lie i' th' earth ere he rot?

FIRST CLOWN: I' faith, if he be not rotten before he die, (as we have many pocky corses nowadays, that will scarce hold the laying in) he will last you some eight year, or nine year. A tanner will last you nine year.

HAMLET: Why he, more than another?

FIRST CLOWN: Why sir, his hide is so tann'd with his trade, that he will keep out water a great while. And your water, is a sore decayer of your whoreson dead body. Here's a skull now: this skull, has lain in the earth three and twenty years.

HAMLET: Whose was it?

FIRST CLOWN: A whoreson mad fellow's it was; whose do you think it was?

HAMLET: Nay, I know not.

FIRST CLOWN: A pestilence on him for a mad rogue, a' pour'd a flagon of Rhenish on my head once. This same skull sir, this same skull sir, was Yorick's skull, the King's Jester.

HAMLET: This?

FIRST CLOWN: E'en that.

HAMLET: Let me see. Alas poor Yorick, I knew him Horatio, a fellow of infinite jest; of most excellent fancy, he hath borne me on his back a thousand times: and now how abhorred in my imagination it is, my gorge rises at it. Here hung those lips, that I have kiss'd I know not how oft. Where be your gibes now? your gambols? your songs? your flashes of merriment that were wont to set the table on a roar? Not one now to mock your own jeering? quite chop-fallen? Now get you to my Lady's chamber, and tell her, let her paint an inch thick, to this favour she must come. Make her laugh at that: prithee Horatio tell me one thing.

HORATIO: What's that my Lord?

HAMLET: Dost thou think Alexander look'd o' this fashion i' th' earth?

HORATIO: E'en so.

HAMLET: And smelt so? puh.

HORATIO: E'en so, my Lord.

HAMLET: To what base uses we may return, Horatio Why may not imagination trace the noble dust of Alexander, till he find it stopping a bung-hole?

HORATIO: 'Twere to consider too curiously, to consider so.

HAMLET: No faith, not a jot. But to follow him thither with modesty enough, and likelihood to lead it; as thus. Alexander died: Alexander was buried: Alexander returned! into dust; the dust is earth; of earth we make loam, and why of that loam (whereto he was converted) might they not stop a beer-barrel?

Imperial Cæsar, dead and turn'd to clay.
Might stop a hole to keep the wind away.
O, that that earth, which kept the world in awe,
Should patch a wall, t' expel the winter's flaw.

But soft, but soft, aside; here comes the King.

Enter bearers with a Coffin, the King and Queen, Laertes and other Lords, a Priest following.

The Queen, the courtiers. Who is that they follow,
And with such maimed rites? This doth betoken,
The corse they follow, did with desperate hand,
Fordo its own life; 'twas of some estate.
Couch we awhile, and mark.

LAERTES: What ceremony else?

HAMLET: That is Laertes, a very noble youth: mark.

LAERTES: What ceremony else?

PRIEST: Her obsequies have been as far enlarg'd.
As we have warrantise, her death was doubtful,
And but that great command o'ersways the order,
She should in ground unsanctified have lodg'd,
Till the last Trumpet. For charitable prayer,
Shards, flints, and pebbles, should be thrown on her:
Yet here she is allow'd her virgin rites,
Her maiden strewments, and the bringing home
Of bell and burial.

LAERTES: Must there no more be done?

PRIEST: No more be done:
We should profane the service of the dead,
To sing sage *requiem*, and such rest to her
As to peace-parted souls.

LAERTES: Lay her i' th' earth,
And from her fair and unpolluted flesh,
May violets spring. I tell thee (churlish priest)
A ministering angel shall my sister be,
When thou liest howling.
HAMLET: What, the fair Ophelia?
QUEEN: Sweets to the sweet, farewell.
I hop'd thou shouldst have been my Hamlet's wife:
I thought thy bride-bed to have deck'd (sweet maid)
And not have strew'd thy grave.
LAERTES: O treble woe,
Fall ten times treble on that cursed head
Whose wicked deed thy most ingenious sense
Depriv'd thee of. Hold off the earth awhile,
Till I have caught her once more in mine arms:

Leaps into the grave.

Now pile your dust, upon the quick, and dead,
Till of this flat a mountain you have made,
To o'ertop old Pelion, or the skyish head
Of blue Olympus.
HAMLET: What is he, whose griefs
Bear such an emphasis? whose phrase of sorrow
Conjures the wandering stars, and makes them stand
Like wonder-wounded hearers? This is I,
Hamlet the Dane.

Hamlet leaps in after Laertes.

LAERTES: The devil take thy soul.
HAMLET: Thou pray'st not well:
I prithee take thy fingers from my throat;
Sir, though I am not splenitive, and rash,
Yet have I something in me dangerous,
Which let thy wiseness fear. Away thy hand.
KING: Pluck them asunder.
QUEEN: Hamlet, Hamlet.

HORATIO: Good my Lord, be quiet.

HAMLET: Why I will fight with him upon this theme
Until my eyelids will no longer wag.

QUEEN: O my son, what theme?

HAMLET: I lov'd Ophelia; forty thousand brothers
Could not (with all their quantity of love)
Make up my sum. What wilt thou do for her?

KING: O he is mad Laertes.

QUEEN: For love of God forbear him.

HAMLET: Come show me what thou'lt do.
Woo't weep? woo't fight? woo't fast? woo't tear thyself?
Woo't drink up eisel, eat a crocodile?
I'll do't. Dost thou come here to whine;
To outface me with leaping in her grave?
Be buried quick with her, and so will I.
And if thou prate of mountains; let them throw
Millions of acres on us; till our ground
Singeing his pate against the burning zone,
Make Ossa like a wart. Nay, and thou'lt mouth,
I'll rant as well as thou.

QUEEN: This is mere madness:
And thus awhile the fit will work on him:
Anon as patient as the female dove,
When that her golden couplets are disclosed,
His silence will sit drooping.

HAMLET: Hear you sir:
What is the reason that you use me thus?
I lov'd you ever; but it is no matter:
Let Hercules himself do what he may,
The cat will mew, and dog will have his day.

Exit.

KING: I pray you good Horatio wait upon him:

Exit Horatio.

Strengthen your patience in our last night's speech,
We'll put the matter to the present push:
Good Gertrude set some watch over your son,
This grave shall have a living monument:
An hour of quiet shortly shall we see;
Till then, in patience our proceeding be.

Exeunt.

V.2

Enter Hamlet and Horatio.

HAMLET: So much for this sir; now shall you see the other, You do remember all the circumstance?
HORATIO: Remember it my Lord?
HAMLET: Sir, in my heart there was a kind of fighting,
That would not let me sleep; methought I lay
Worse than the mutines in the bilboes, rashly,
(And praised be rashness for it, let us know,
Our indiscretion sometimes serves us well,
When our deep plots do pall, and that should teach us,
There's a Divinity that shapes our ends,
Rough-hew them how we will) —
HORATIO: This is most certain.
HAMLET: Up from my cabin
My sea-gown scarf'd about me in the dark,
Grop'd I to find out them; had my desire,
Finger'd their packet, and in fine, withdrew
To mine own room again, making so bold,
(My fears forgetting manners) to unseal
Their grand commission, where I found Horatio,
Oh royal knavery: an exact command,
Larded with many several sorts of reasons;

Importing Denmark's health, and England's too,
With hoo, such bugs and goblins in my life,
That on the supervise no leisure bated,
No not to stay the grinding of the axe,
My head should be struck off.

HORATIO: Is't possible?

HAMLET: Here's the commission, read it at more leisure:
But wilt thou hear me how I did proceed?

HORATIO: I beseech you.

HAMLET: Being thus be-netted round with villains,
Or I could make a prologue to my brains,
They had begun the play. I sate me down,
Devis'd a new commission, wrote it fair,
I once did hold it as our statists do,
A baseness to write fair: and labour'd much
How to forget that learning: but sir now,
It did me yeoman's service: wilt thou know
The effects of what I wrote?

HORATIO: Ay, good my Lord.

HAMLET: An earnest conjuration from the King,
As England was his faithful tributary,
As love between them, as the palm should flourish,
As Peace should still her wheaten garland wear,
And stand a comma 'tween their amities,
And many such-like As'es of great charge,
That on the view and know of these contents,
Without debatement further, more or less,
He should the bearers put to sudden death,
Not shriving-time allow'd.

HORATIO: How was this seal'd?

HAMLET: Why, even in that was Heaven ordinate;
I had my father's signet in my purse,
Which was the model of that Danish seal:
Folded the writ up in form of the other,
Subscrib'd it, gave't th' impression, plac'd it safely,

The changeling never known: now, the next day
Was our sea-fight, and what to this was sequent.
Thou know'st already.

HORATIO: So Guildenstern and Rosencrantz, go to't.

HAMLET: Why man, they did make love to this employment.
They are not near my conscience; their defeat
Doth by their own insinuation grow:
'Tis dangerous, when the baser nature comes
Between the pass, and fell incensed points
Of mighty opposites.

HORATIO. Why, what a King is this?

HAMLET: Does it not, thinks't thee, stand me now upon?
He that hath kill'd my King, and whor'd my mother,
Popp'd in between th' election and my hopes,
Thrown out his angle for my proper life.
And with such cozenage; is't not perfect conscience,
To quit him with this arm? and is't not to be damn'd
To let this canker of our nature come?
In further evil?

HORATIO: It must be shortly known to him from England what is the issue of the business there.

HAMLET: It will be short,
The interim's mine, and a man's life's no more
Than to say one: but I am very sorry good Horatio,
That to Laertes I forgot myself;
For by the image of my cause, I see
The portraiture of his; I'll court his favours:
But sure the bravery of his grief did put me
Into a towering passion.

HORATIO: Peace, who comes here?

Enter young Osric.

OSRIC: Your Lordship is right welcome back to Denmark.

HAMLET: I humbly thank you sir, dost know this waterfly?

HORATIO: No my good Lord.

HAMLET: Thy state is the more gracious; for 'tis a vice to know him: he hath much land, and fertile; let a beast be Lord of beasts, and his crib shall stand at the King's mess; 'tis a chough; but as I say, spacious in the possession of dirt.

OSRIC: Sweet Lord, if your friendship were at leisure, I should impart a thing to you from his Majesty.

HAMLET: I will receive it with all diligence of spirit; put your bonnet to his right use, 'tis for the head.

OSRIC: I thank your Lordship, it is very hot.

HAMLET: No, believe me 'tis very cold, the wind is northerly.

OSRIC: It is indifferent cold my Lord indeed.

HAMLET: Methinks it is very sultry, and hot for my complexion.

OSRIC: Exceedingly, my Lord, it is very sultry, as 'twere I cannot tell how: but my Lord, his Majesty bade me signify to you, that he has laid a great wager on your head: sir, this is the matter.

HAMLET: I beseech you remember.

OSRIC: Nay, in good faith, for mine ease in good faith: [sir here is newly come to Court Laertes, believe me an absolute gentleman, full of most excellent differences, of very soft society, and great showing: indeed to speak feelingly of him, he is the card or calendar of gentry: fear you shall find in him the continent of what part a gentleman would see.

HAMLET: Sir, his definement suffers no perdition in you, though I know to divide him inventorially would dizzy th' arithmetic of memory, and yet but yaw neither in respect of his quick sail, but in the verity of extolment, I take him to be a soul of great article, and his infusion of such dearth and rareness, as to make true diction of him, his semblable is his mirror, and who else would trace him, his umbrage nothing more.

OSRIC: Your Lordship speaks most infallibly of him.

HAMLET: The concernancy sir, why do we wrap the gentleman in our more rawer breath?

OSRIC: Sir.

HORATIO: Is't not possible to understand in another tongue, you will to't sir really.

HAMLET: What imports the nomination of this gentleman?

OSRIC: Of Laertes?

HORATIO: His purse is empty already, all's golden words are spent.

HAMLET: Of him sir.

OSRIC: I know you are not ignorant.

HAMLET: I would you did sir, yet in faith if you did, it would not much approve me, well sir?]

OSRIC: You are not ignorant of what excellence Laertes is.

[HAMLET: I dare not confess that, lest I should compare with him in excellence, but to know a man well, were to know himself.

OSRIC: I mean sir for his weapon, but in the imputation laid on him, by them in his meed, he's unfellowed.]

HAMLET: What's his weapon?

OSRIC: Rapier and dagger.

HAMLET: That's two of his weapons; but well.

OSRIC: The King sir has wager'd with him six Barbary horses, against the which he impon'd as I take it, six French rapiers and poniards, with their assigns, as girdle, hangers or so: three of the carriages in faith are very dear to fancy, very responsive to the hilts, most delicate carriages, and of very liberal conceit.

HAMLET: What call you the carriages?

[HORATIO: I knew you must be edified by the margent ere you had done.]

OSRIC: The carriages sir, are the hangers.

HAMLET: The phrase would be more germane to the matter, if we could carry cannon by our sides; I would it might be hangers till then; but on, six Barbary horses against six French swords, their assigns, and three liberal-conceited carriages, that's the French bet against the Danish, why is this impon'd as you call it?

OSRIC: The King sir, hath laid that in a dozen passes between yourself and him, he shall not exceed you three hits; he hath laid on twelve for nine, and that would come to immediate trial, if your Lordship would vouchsafe the answer.

HAMLET: How if I answer no?

OSRIC: I mean my Lord, the opposition of your person in trial.

HAMLET: Sir, I will walk here in the Hall; if it please his Majesty, it is the breathing time of day with me; let the foils be brought, the gentleman willing, and the King hold his purpose; I will win for him if I can: if not, I will gain nothing but my shame, and the odd hits.

OSRIC: Shall I redeliver you e'en so?

HAMLET: To this effect sir, after what flourish your nature will.

OSRIC: I commend my duty to your Lordship.

Exit.

HAMLET: Yours, yours; he does well to commend it himself, there are no tongues else for's turn.

HORATIO: This lapwing runs away with the shell on his head.

HAMLET: He did comply with his dug before he suck'd it: thus has he and many more of the same bevy that I know the drossy age dotes on, only got the tune of the time, and outward habit of encounter, a kind of yesty collection, which carries them through and through the most fond and winnowed opinions; and do *but blow* them to their trials: the bubbles are out.

[*Enter a Lord.*

LORD: My Lord, his Majesty commended him to you by young Osric, who brings back to him that you attend him in the Hall He sends to know if your pleasure hold to play with Laertes, or that you will take longer time?

HAMLET: I am constant to my purposes, they follow the King's pleasure, if his fitness speaks, mine is ready; now or whensoever, provided I be so able as now.

LORD: The King, and Queen, and all are coming down.

HAMLET: In happy time.

LORD: The Queen desires you to use some gentle entertainment to Laertes, before you fall to play.

HAMLET: She well instructs me.

Exit Lord.]

HORATIO: You will lose this wager, my Lord.

HAMLET: I do not think so, since he went into France, I have been in continual practice; I shall win at the odds: but thou wouldst not think how ill all's here about my heart: but it is no matter.

HORATIO: Nay, good my Lord.

HAMLET: It is but foolery; but it is such a kind of gain-giving, as would perhaps trouble a woman.

HORATIO: If your mind dislike any thing, obey. I will forestal their repair hither, and say you are not fit.

HAMLET: Not a whit, we defy augury; there is special providence in the fall of a sparrow. If it be now, 'tis not to come: if it be not to come, it will be now: if it be not now, yet it will come; the readiness is all, since no man has aught of what he leaves. What is't to leave betimes?

Enter trumpets, drums and officer with cushion; King, Queen, and all the State; Attendants with foils and daggers; Laertes; a table prepared and flagons of wine on it.

KING: Come Hamlet, come, and take this hand from me.

HAMLET: Give me your pardon sir, I've done you wrong,
But pardon't as you are a gentleman.
This presence knows,
And you must needs have heard how I am punish'd
With sore distraction? What I have done
That might your nature, honour and exception
Roughly awake, I here proclaim was madness:
Was't Hamlet wrong'd Laertes? Never Hamlet.
If Hamlet from himself be ta'en away:
And when he's not himself, does wrong Laertes,
Then Hamlet does it not, Hamlet denies it:
Who does it then? His madness. If't be so,

Hamlet is of the faction that is wrong'd,
His madness is poor Hamlet's enemy.
Sir, in this audience,
Let my disclaiming from a purpos'd evil,
Free me so far in your most generous thoughts,
That I have shot mine arrow o'er the house,
And hurt my brother.

LAERTES: I am satisfied in Nature,
Whose motive in this case should stir me most
To my revenge. But in my terms of Honour
I stand aloof, and will no reconcilement,
Till by some elder masters of known honour,
I have a voice, and precedent of peace
To keep my name ungor'd. But till that time,
I do receive your offer'd love like love,
And will not wrong it.

HAMLET: I do embrace it freely,
And will this brother's wager frankly play.
Give us the foils: come on.

LAERTES: Come, one for me.

HAMLET: I'll be your foil Laertes, in mine ignorance
Your skill shall like a star i' th' darkest night,
Stick fiery off indeed.

LAERTES: You mock me sir.

HAMLET: No by this hand.

KING: Give them the foils young Osric, Cousin Hamlet.
You know the wager.

HAMLET: Very well my Lord,
Your Grace hath laid the odds a' th' weaker side.

KING: I do not fear it, I have seen you both:
But since he is better'd, we have therefore odds.

LAERTES: This is too heavy, let,me see another.

HAMLET: This likes me well, these foils have all a length.

They prepare to play.

OSRIC: Ay my good Lord.

KING: Set me the stoups of wine upon that table:
If Hamlet give the first, or second hit,
Or quit in answer of the third exchange,
Let all the battlements their ordnance fire,
The King shall drink to Hamlet's better breath,
And in the cup an union shall he throw
Richer than that, which four successive Kings
In Denmark's Crown have worn. Give me the cups.
And let the kettle to the trumpets speak,
The trumpet to the cannoneer without,
The cannons to the heavens, the heaven to earth,
Now the King drinks to Hamlet. Come, begin,
And you the judges bear a wary eye.

Trumpets the while.

HAMLET: Come on sir.

LAERTES: Come my Lord.

They play.

HAMLET: One.

LAERTES: No.

HAMLET: Judgement.

OSRIC: A hit, a very palpable hit.

LAERTES: Well: again.

KING: Stay, give me drink. Hamlet, this pearl is thine, Here's to thy health. Give him the cup.

Drums, trumpets and shot. Flourish. A piece goes off.

HAMLET: I'll play this bout first, set by awhile.
Come: another hit; what say you?

LAERTES: A touch, a touch, I do confess.

KING: Our son shall win.

QUEEN: He's fat, and scant of breath.
Here Hamlet take my napkin, rub thy brows:
The Queen carouses to thy fortune, Hamlet.

HAMLET: Good Madam.

KING: Gertrude, do not drink.

QUEEN: I will my Lord; I pray you pardon me.

KING: It is the poison'd cup, it is too late.

HAMLET: I dare not drink yet Madam, by and by.

QUEEN: Come, let me wipe thy face.

LAERTES: My Lord, I'll hit him now.

KING: I do not think't.

LAERTES: And yet it is almost against my conscience.

HAMLET: Come for the third. Laertes, you but dally,
I pray you pass with your best violence,
I am afear'd you make a wanton of me.

LAERTES: Say you so? come on.

They play.

OSRIC: Nothing neither way.

LAERTES: Have at you now.

In scuffling they catch one another's rapiers and both are wounded.

KING: Part them, they are incens'd.

HAMLET: Nay come, again.

Laertes falls down; the Queen falls down, dying.

OSRIC: Look to the Queen there hoa.

HORATIO: They bleed on both sides. How is't my Lord?

OSRIC: How is't Laertes.

LAERTES: Why as a woodcock to mine own springe,
Osric, I am justly kill'd with mine own treachery.

HAMLET: How does the Queen?

KING: She sounds to see them bleed.

QUEEN: No, no, the drink, the drink. O my dear
Hamlet, The drink, the drink, I am poison'd.

Dies.

HAMLET: O villainy! How? let the door be lock'd.
Treachery, seek it out.

LAERTES: It is here Hamlet. Hamlet, thou art slain,
No medicine in the world can do thee good.
In thee, there is not half an hour of life;
The treacherous instrument is in thy hand,
Unbated and envenom'd: the foul practice
Hath turn'd itself on me. Lo, here I lie,
Never to rise again: thy mother's poison'd:
I can no more, the King, the King's to blame.

HAMLET: The point envenom'd too,
Then venom to thy work

Stabs the King.

ALL: Treason, treason.

KING: O yet defend me friends, I am but hurt.

HAMLET: Here thou incestuous, murderous, damned Dane,
Drink off this potion: is thy union here?
Follow my mother.

King dies.

LAERTES: He is justly serv'd.
It is a poison temper'd by himself:
Exchange forgiveness with me, noble Hamlet;
Mine and my father's death come not upon thee,
Nor thine on me.

Dies.

HAMLET: Heaven make thee free of it, I follow thee.
I am dead Horatio, wretched Queen adieu.
You look that pale, and tremble at this chance,
That are but mutes or audience to this act:
Had I but time (as this fell Sergeant Death
Is strict in his arrest) O I could tell you.
But let it be: Horatio, I am dead,
Thou liv'st, report me and my cause aright

To the unsatisfied.

HORATIO: Never believe it.
I am more an antique Roman than a Dane:
Here's yet some liquor left.

HAMLET: As th'art a man,
Give me the cup. Let go, by Heaven I'll have't.
O good Horatio, what a wounded name,
(Things standing thus unknown) shall live behind me.
If thou didst ever hold me in thy heart,
Absent thee from felicity awhile,
And in this harsh world draw thy breath in pain,
To tell my story.

March afar off, and shot within.

What warlike noise is this?

Enter Osric.

OSRIC: Young Fortinbras, with conquest come from Poland
To th' Ambassadors of England gives
This warlike volley.

HAMLET: O I die Horatio :
The potent poison quite o'er-crows my spirit,
I cannot live to hear the news from England,
But I do prophesy th' election lights
On Fortinbras, he has my dying voice
So tell him with the occurrents more and less,
Which have solicited. The rest is silence.

Dies.

HORATIO: Now cracks a noble heart: good night sweet Prince,
And flights of Angels sing thee to thy rest.
Why does the drum come hither?

Enter Fortinbras and English Ambassadors, with drums, colours, and Attendants.

FORTINBRAS: Where is this sight?

HORATIO: What is it you would see;

If aught of woe, or wonder, cease your search.
FORTINBRAS: This quarry cries on havoc. O proud death,
What feast is toward in thine eternal cell,
That thou so many Princes, at a shot,
So bloodily hast struck?
FIRST AMBASSADOR: The sight is dismal,
And our affairs from England come too late,
The ears are senseless that should give us hearing,
To tell him his commandment is fulfill'd,
That Rosencrantz and Guildenstern are dead:
Where should we have our thanks?
HORATIO: Not from his mouth,
Had it th' ability of life to thank you:
He never gave commandment for their death.
But since so jump upon this bloody question,
You from the Polack wars, and you from England
Are here arriv'd, give order that these bodies
High on a stage be placed to the view,
And let me speak to th' yet unknowing world,
How these things came about. So shall you hear
Of carnal, bloody, and unnatural acts,
Of accidental judgements, casual slaughters,
Of deaths put on by cunning, and forc'd cause,
And in this upshot, purposes mistook,
Fall'n on the inventors' heads. All this can I Truly deliver.
FORTINBRAS: Let us haste to hear it,
And call the noblest to the audience.
For me, with sorrow, I embrace my fortune,
I have some rights of memory in this Kingdom,
Which now to claim my vantage doth invite me,
HORATIO: Of that I shall have also cause to speak,
And from his mouth whose voice will draw no more:
But let this same be presently perform'd,
Even while men's minds are wild, lest some mischance

On plots, and errors happen.
FORTINBRAS: Let four captains
Bear Hamlet like a soldier to the stage,
For he was likely, had he been put on
To have prov'd most royally: and for his passage,
The soldiers' music, and the rites of war
Speak loudly for him.
Take up the body; such a sight as this
Becomes the field, but here shows much amiss.
Go, bid the soldiers shoot.

Exeunt marching: after the which a peal of ordnance are shot off.

GLOSSARY

abridgement: pastime,
additional: honour.
admiration: wonder, astonishment.
aery: nest.
affection: affection,
anchor: anchorite, hermit.
amble: walk affectedly.
angle: rod and line.
annexment: attachment.
antic disposition: pretended madness.
appurtenance: that which belongs to.
argument: plot of a play.
arras: tapestry hanging.
arter: artery.
at point exactly: at all points, complete.

barr'd: thwarted.
bated: abated.
bedded: lying flat.
beetles: juts.
beshrew: plague on.
bespeak: command.
beteem: allow.
bisson: blind.
blank: target.
blown youth: youth in full bloom.
bodkin: dagger.
bodykins: little body.
bourne: boundary.
brainish: mad.
braz'd: covered with brass.
breath: utterance.
breathing time: time for exercise.
brokers: go-betweens.
buttons: buds.
buz, buz: stale news.

canon: law.
canopy: covering.
canker: maggot.
cap-a-pe: from head to foot.
capable: capable of feeling.
cataplasm: plaster.
cautel: craft.
censure: opinion.
chapless: without cheeks.
character: (a) handwriting, (b) write.
chough: jackdaw.
clepe: call.
climature: climate, country.
coil: turmoil.

collateral: related, accessory.
comply with: use ceremony with.
compost: manure.
conceit: Imagination.
compounded: mixed.
condolement: lamentation.
conjunctive: inseparable.
consequence: sequel.
consummation: conclusion.
continent: able to contain.
contraction: contract of marriage.
convoy: means of conveyance.
coped: encountered.
coted: came alongside.
couch: lie down.
cousin: kinsman.
counter: follow the scent in the wrong direction.
counterfeit presentment: portrait.
crowner: coroner.

Danskers: Danes.
declension: downward path.
discourse of reason: power of reason.
distemper'd: disturbed.
dole: grief.
distilled: melted.
distract: out of her mind.
doublet: short, close-fitting coat
doubt: suspect
douts: puts out
down-gyved: hanging like fetters round his ankles.
drift of question: indirect inquiry.
drossy: scummy.
dupped: opened.

ecstasy: madness.
effects: material advantages.
eisel: vinegar.
emulate: emulous, jealous.
enactures: resolutions.
encompassments: circumlocution.
encumbered: folded.
entertainment: welcome hospitality.
entreatments: preliminary conversations.
escoted: paid.
espiels: spies.
even: straight
even Christian: fellow Christian.
extent: outward show.
extorted: evilly acquired.
extravagant: wandering.
eyases: hawks.

faction: party.
fantasy: imagination, illusion.
fardels: burdens.
fat: out of condition.
favour: face, appearance.

fay: faith.
féats: acts.
fellies: rim of a wheel
flats: low-lying shore.
flushing: filling with water.
fordo: destroy.
foreknowing: foreknowledge.
forms: mental images.
free: guiltless.
fretted: ornamented.
friending: friendliness.
function: action, behaviour.
fust: grow musty.

gaged: pledged.
gate: bitterness.
gain-giving: misgiving.
gait: progress.
general gender: the people at large.
generous: of gentle birth.
gentry: gentlemanly behaviour.
germane: relative.
gib: tomcat.
God buy: God be with.
God 'ild you: God reward you.
gorge: throat.
grizzled: grey.
gross and scope: full view.
gules: red in the jargon of heraldry.
gulf: whirlpool.
gyves: fetters.

habit: garments.
hangers: straps for carrying the sword.
happily: haply.
harrows: distresses.
hearsed: buried.
heat: anger.
he benon: probably henbane.
hectic: fever.
hic et ubique: here and everywhere.
honest: chaste.
hoodman blind: blind man's buff.
hugger-mugger: 'anyhow', i.e. in secret haste.
husbandry: economy.
Hyperion: the Sun.
Hyrcanian beast: the tiger.

idle: silly.
Ilium: the citadel of Troy.
impasted: encrusted.
imponed: pawned, bet.
imposthume: a boil.
impress: conscription.
incorps'd: of one body with.
incorrect to: unruled by.
Inhibition: prohibition.
infants: buds.
instances: motives.
inurned: buried.
investments: outward garments.
it: its.

jig: dance wantonly.
jointress: partner.
journeyman: hired workman.
jowls: claps down.
jump: immediately.
just: exactly.

keep: live.
kettle: kettle drum.
kindless: unnatural.

larded: garnished.
large discourse: power of reasoning.
lazar-like: like leprosy.
lenten: fasting, meagre.
lets: hinders.
liberal conceit: elaborate pattern.
lighted: alighted.
loose: torn loose.
luxury: lust.

made probation: proved to be true.
mazzard: pate.
meed: merit.
merely: utterly.
miching mallecho: slinking mischief
milch: moist.
mobled: muffled.
moiety competent: adequate share.
mope: be dull.
moth: mote, speck of dust
mouse: a term of affection.
mows: insulting grimaces.
murdering-pieces: cannon loaded with grape-shot.

nave: centre of a wheel.
nonce: for the once, occasion.
occulted: concealed.
o'erraught: overtook.
o'er-sized: painted over.
o'er-teemed: exhausted by bearing children.
omen: disaster.
operant: active.
opposite: obstacle.
overpeering of his list: overstepping its boundary.
outstretched: exaggerated.

paddock: toad.
painted: motionless as in a picture.
painting: imitation.
pajock: peacock.
pales: defences.
pall: fail.
passages of proof: experiences that prove.
performed at height: achieved greatly.
peak: mope.
pioner: engineer, or military miner.

plausive: pleasing.
pith: marrow.
plurisy: excess.
policy: state craft.
porpentine: porcupine.
posset: curdle.
powers: forces.
precurse: forerunner.
pregnant: ready, apt.
prenominate: aforesaid.
prescripts: commands.
presently: immediately.
pressure: impression, imprint of a seal.
prevent: forestall.
primy nature: nature in its spring time.
process: procedure.
property of easiness: a matter of indifference.
pursy: puffy.

quaintly: skilfully.
quality: acting profession.
quit: repay.
quoted: noted.

rack: the cloud in the sky.
range: run about.
rank: overgrown.
ranker: richer.
razed: ornamented with cuts.
reach: far sight.
recorder: a wood-wind instrument.
reechy: grimy.
remorse: pity.
replication: echo.
resolve: melt.
respect: consideration.
responsive to: matching well.
retrograde: contrary.
rhapsody: meaningless sound.
rheum: moisture.
riband: ribbon.
rivals: partners.
romage: literally, clearing out the hold of a ship.
rouse: deep draught, carouse.
row: line.

sable: black.
sallets: piquancies.
sanctified: sanctimonious.
saws: wise sayings.
school: university.
scrimers: fencers.
sealed: confirmed the election.
season: (a) qualify, (b) ripen.
secure hour: hour of ease.
seized of: possessed of.
sensible: perceived by the senses.
shark'd up: collected indiscriminately.
sheeted: shrouded.
shent: rebuked.
shoon: shoes.
siege: seat, and so rank, importance.

sold in fee: freehold.
sort: (a) fall out, (b) reckon.
sounds: swoons.
splenitive: hot tempered.
springe: snare.
stamp of nature: the impression made by
nature: natural character.
station: noble bearing.
statists: statesmen.
still: ever, continuously.
stithy: smithy.
stomach: requiring courage.
stoup: large drinking cup.
stuck: thrust.
subject: subjects.
sullies (spelt *sallies* in the Second Quarto): blemishes.
suppliance of a minute: momentary.
supposed: estimation.
Switzers: Swiss body-guard.
Swounds: by God's wounds.

taints: blemishes.
takes: bewitches.
tone on: set on.
tax'd: censured.
temple: i.e. the body.
tempered: mixed.
tend: attend.
tender: (a) offer, (b) counter.
tent: probe.
touch'd: implicated.
tricked: heraldic word for painted.
umbrage: shadow.
unbated: unblunted, sharp.
unction: ointment.
uneffectual: made powerless.
unfortified: irreligious.
ungracious: graceless.
unimproved: unschooled, rash.
union: pearl.
unpregnant: having no living thought within.
unproportioned: unsuitable.
unreclaimed: untouched, naturally wild.
unsifted: untried.
unsinew'd: nerveless.
up-spring: a wild dance.

vailed: lowered.
valanced: fringed, i.e. with a beard.
variable: varied.
varnish: gloss.
ventages: stops in the recorder.
vigour: violent action.
voice: vote.

windlasses: winding about.

yaw: sail unsteadily.
yesty collection: frothy knowledge.